NEGOTIATING JUSTICE

A NEW CONSTITUTION
FOR SOUTH AFRICA

NEGOTIATING JUSTICE

A NEW CONSTITUTION FOR SOUTH AFRICA

EDITED BY

MERVYN BENNUN

AND

MALYN D.D. NEWITT

UNIVERSITY
of
EXETER
PRESS

First published in 1995 by
University of Exeter Press
Reed Hall, Streatham Drive
Exeter EX4 4QR
UK

www.exeterpress.co.uk

© Mervyn Bennun and Malyn D.D. Newitt
and the several authors, each in respect of the
material contributed 1995

A catalogue record for this book is available from the British Library.

ISBN 9780859894593

Contents

Notes on Contributors vi

Chapter One
Introduction
Malyn Newitt 1

Chapter Two
Understanding the Nightmare:
Politics and Violence in South Africa
Mervyn E. Bennun 26

Chapter Three
Constitution-Making:
In Search of a Democratic South Africa
Nico Steytler 62

Chapter Four
A Bill of Rights as an Instrument for Social and Economic
Transformation in a New South African Constitution:
Lessons from India
Pierre de Vos 81

Chapter Five
The Protection of Property in South Africa
Andrew Caiger 113

Chapter Six
Legislating for Peace:
An Overview of Attempts to Promote Peace in South Africa
J. R. Midgley 141

Chapter Seven
Conclusion
Malyn Newitt and Mervyn Bennun 177

Index 196

Notes on Contributors

MALYN NEWITT is Senior Lecturer in History at Exeter University. He was a lecturer at the University of Rhodesia in the 1960s and is author of a number of books on the Portuguese colonies in Africa. These include *Portuguese Settlement on the Zambesi*, *Portugal in Africa: the Last Hundred Years*, *Sao Tomé and Príncipe* (with Tony Hodges), and *A History of Mozambique*. He has also written a book on the Comoros Islands and has edited volumes on the English Civil War, the early history of the Portuguese empire and the political economy of tropical islands.

MERVYN BENNUN graduated from the University of Cape Town with BA, LLB in 1960 and practised at the Bar in Port Elizabeth and Cape Town until 1965. He completed an LLM at the London School of Economics in 1967, and after a period working as a research assistant at the LSE and for JUSTICE (the British section of the International Commission of Jurists) he became a lecturer in the Law Department at the University of Exeter in 1968, where he has specialised in criminal law, criminology, artificial intelligence and expert systems, and legal process. He was a visiting lecturer in Law at the University of the Western Cape during 1991. Publications include the Table of Contents and Index to *The African Communist*, 1958-1988 (Inkululeko Publications), covering the first 30 years of publication; as editor, *Computers, Artificial Intelligence and the Law*; as co-editor, *Law, Computer Science and Artificial Intelligence*, 'The Judiciary in Franco's Spain and in South Africa: A Comparison' in *Civil Rights, Public Opinion, and the State* (European Group for the Study of Deviance and Social Control), 'Witnesses for the Prosecution in South Africa: Some Comments' (in *Acta Juridica*), and papers on criminal law.

The Contributors

NICO STEYTLER, BA, LLB (Stellenbosch) LLM (London), PhD (Natal), is Senior Professor of Law and Acting Director of the Community Law Centre, University of the Western Cape. He was also Chairperson of the Department of Public and Adjective Law, University of the Western Cape from 1989-93. Previously he was Professor of Law, University of Natal, Durban. His research has focused mainly on the administration of criminal justice in South Africa, and recently the scope has widened to include a number of topics in the field of constitutional law. Publications include the following books: as co-editor of *Criminal Justice in South Africa* (1983), *The Undefended Accused on Trial* (1988), editor of *The Freedom Charter and Beyond: Founding Principles for a Democratic South African Legal Order* (1991), co-author with Hugh Corder *et al.*, *A Charter for Social Justice: A Contribution to the South African Bill of Rights Debate* (1992), co-editor of *Free and Fair Elections* (1994).

PIERRE DE VOS completed a BComm (Law) and a LLB degree at the University of Stellenbosch. He studied at Columbia University in New York where he obtained an LLM degree, specialising in constitutional law. He also completed an LLM dissertation on directive principles in the Indian constitution at the University of Stellenbosch. He was the co-editor of *Free and Fair Elections* which was published in the run-up to South Africa's first democratic election. He presently lectures in constitutional law and criminal law at the University of the Western Cape.

ANDREW CAIGER is Senior Lecturer in Law at Anglia Polytechnic University. He read law at the University of Cape Town and for the MA in Industrial Relations at the Warwick Business School, Warwick University. He taught law at the Universities of Transkei and Bophuthatswana before moving to the United Kingdom. He has presented several papers in the United Kingdom at the WG Hart Legal Workshop and the Socio-Legal Studies Association annual meetings, and at several Law & Society Meetings in the United States on South African human rights and constitutional issues. He is currently engaged on research into cause-lawyers in South Africa. Other areas of research include dispute resolution within the construction industry and re-insurance. His recent publications include 'Lawyers and Arbitration: The Juridification of Construction Disputes' (with John Flood).

ROB MIDGLEY is a Professor of Law at Rhodes University, Grahamstown and an Advocate of the Supreme Court of South Africa. His interests include criminal justice and the provision of legal services and he is particularly interested in finding appropriate methods for managing disputes.

As a member of the Grahamstown Peace Committee and Independent Mediation Services (IMSSA) panellist he has mediated various community disputes and is actively involved in restoring police/community relations in South Africa. He served as chairperson of a commission which looked into the provision of policing services in Grahamstown and currently serves as an executive member of the Grahamstown Community/Police Consultation Forum. He is an accredited National Peace Accord trainer in conflict management. During the recent elections he worked for the Independent Electoral Commission as a Deputy Provincial Director for its Monitoring Division. In 1993 he received the Vice-Chancellor's Research Award from Rhodes University.

Chapter One

Introduction

Malyn Newitt

The reform of an autocratic state is a notoriously difficult process. Anyone aware of the history of Europe in the last two hundred years will immediately recall Alexis de Tocqueville's famous phrase 'the most dangerous moment for a bad government is generally that in which it sets about reform'.[1] It is as though the rigid structure of a dam is breached and the force of pent-up waters thus released sweep away the remnants of the dam and demolish all the lesser structures in its path.

Seen in retrospect the decolonisation carried out by Britain and France in the early 1960s is a remarkable exception. There was no bursting of the dam. The authoritarian, multi-ethnic colonial states were replaced not by democracy but by one party systems which replicated the colonial state to a remarkable extent and transferred authority from a white to a black governing elite. It is fashionable in the early 1990s to denounce the one-party state as a failure and as the cause of all Africa's ills. In many areas even the partial dismantling of the post-colonial state has begun. It is certainly true that many African states proved unable to handle the problems of drought, famine, falling world prices for raw materials and the intolerable pressures of the Cold War, but the post-colonial order in Africa acquired and, thirty years later, still maintains elements of stability which begin to appear more impressive in the light of the rapid disintegration of the post-communist order in USSR and Eastern Europe.

---

1. Alexis de Tocqueville, *The Ancien Regime*, quoted in Rudé G., *Revolutionary*

Negotiating Justice

Whether South Africa will follow the rest of Africa in creating a multi-ethnic, unitary state; or whether it will follow the course set by Yugoslavia, Georgia and Azerbaijan in dissolving into ethnic conflict; or whether it will chart its own path to the future is the subject of endless speculation. This book's contribution to the debate is to present a cogent interpretation of the causes and explanations of communal violence during the 'decolonisation' period from 1990 to April 1994, and of the 'hidden agenda' of the government, and to show how this connects with the political manoeuvring over the new constitution and the debates over entrenching rights in the constitution. Finally the book focuses on the first experiment in creating post-apartheid institutions as a result of the National Peace Accord, and suggests some ways in which the law and legal institutions can create a framework in which communal tension can decrease and underlying problems can be resolved.

1 THE HIDDEN AGENDA OF THE MEN OF VIOLENCE

Most commentators appear to have accepted unquestioningly that following the release of Mandela in 1990 and the establishment of CODESA in December 1991, violence on an unprecedented and ever-increasing scale has engulfed South Africa. Interpreting this violence, and the still more horrific carnage that has taken place in Mozambique and Angola, has become a minor industry among academics and commentators—so much so that Carlos Serra, the professor of History in Maputo University, has acidly condemned intellectuals who play games with the misery caused by violence in Africa 'principally for the opportunity to advance "avant garde" theses irrespective of the political consequences'.[2]

Commentators have, by and large, adopted three approaches, three types of explanation, for the violence in southern Africa. First there are those who place the blame firmly on right-wing forces. For them the violence is orchestrated from outside the black communities and, in the case of Mozambique and Angola, possibly from outside Africa itself,

---

Europe (Fontana, 1964, London) p. 69.
2. Quoted in Wilson, K.B. 'Cults of Violence and Counter-Violence in Mozambique', *Journal of Southern African Studies* (1992) 18: 529

though there is no agreement whether the culprits are the South African government, irresponsible members of the South African security services, a 'third force' made up of extreme right wingers, or foreign based churches, financiers or even fringe politicians.

Secondly, there are those who blame 'tribalism'. They see all African conflict as ultimately rooted in tribal rivalry which the disintegration of colonial or white dominated authoritarian rule has released. Thirdly, there are those who seek socio-economic explanations. For them the violence is the result of social deprivation, of competition for jobs, living space and resources, and of poverty and urbanisation undermining traditional values and restraints and altering accepted gender and generational role models.[3]

In a challenging paper Mervyn Bennun starts by demolishing the point from which virtually all political commentators start—that apartheid came to an end in 1990 and that communal violence is in some way linked to its demise. He is particularly critical of the view that the removal of the state of emergency, the repeal of some of the apartheid Acts and the non-implementation of others has led to the emergence of 'tribal warfare', of atavistic tendencies in the black population, of 'black on black', and increasingly 'black on white' violence. Bennun points out that even those of a liberal persuasion are apparently only too willing to accept this linkage between the 'end of apartheid' and violence, even though they may look for root causes of the violence in social and economic deprivation rather than 'tribalism'.

Bennun's interpretation is fundamentally different. He argues that apartheid has not disappeared, it is merely going through one of its periodic changes of face. It has been pointed out, by Heribert Adam among others, that apartheid (a system of labour control as well as a regime that secured ownership of the land for whites and political power for Afrikaners) was never a rigid, monolithic doctrine adopted by unbending flat-earthers who turned their backs on a changing world. Instead it was a supple ideology which was able to adapt to changing

---

3.   For the debate over the nature of communal violence in South Africa see Chapter 1 of this book, and in addition W. Beinart, 'Political and Collective Violence in Southern African Historiography', *Journal of Southern African Studies* (1992) 18: 455-486 and H. Adam and K. Moodley, 'Political Violence, "Tribalism", and Inkatha', *Journal of Modern African Studies* (1992) 30: 485-510.

circumstances and which avoided the rigidities which at each stage of its existence would have brought it into fatal conflict with superpower and international capitalist interests.[4]

To understand South African history since 1948 one has to see the white (principally Afrikaner) ruling elite as being willing and able to change the face that apartheid turned to the world in order to secure its longer term objectives. Thus the old 'horizontal' apartheid of *baaskap* introduced in 1948 was refurbished by Verwoerd who developed the Homelands policy, with its opportunity for 'vertical' apartheid, at the time when Britain and France were decolonising in the 1960s. South Africa was to be broken up into ten ethnically-based states and black prime ministers, generals and cabinet ministers were to be created, overnight so to speak, in a land where the black population had previously been seen only as hewers of wood and drawers of water and where, as Verwoerd himself had said, there was no room for the black except to perform certain forms of unskilled labour.

The face of apartheid changed but the long-term objectives (cheap, tightly controlled labour, white control over the land and Afrikaner political power) did not. Other changes took place. What had been an Afrikaner nationalist party became a National Party for whites of all origins. An enraged right wing of Afrikaner extremists broke away in 1969 in protest. Industrial job reservation was abandoned; black trades unions were permitted; the pass laws were tinkered with to encourage the emergence of a compliant African middle class. Then in 1983 a new constitution was introduced with roles assigned to coloured and Indian representatives. The idea was to separate these groups from the black opposition and to make apartheid more acceptable to the world. At first this policy appeared to fail. Coloureds and Indians largely rejected the constitution; the Afrikaner community was badly split and the rest of the world was sceptical. Moreover the introduction of the constitution fuelled the fires of black nationalism and led to the insurrection in the townships and the State of Emergency. Nevertheless the Afrikaner politicians who devised the new constitution were 'thinking long'. Ten years later it seems less obvious that their policies were a failure. Indians and coloureds have to a large extent been

---

4. Adam's views have been set out in numerous books and articles; see, for example, *Modernising Racial Domination: South Africa's Political Dynamics* (Berkeley, 1971).

Introduction

detached from the united opposition and in the line-up of forces in the election of April 1994 a clear majority of them offered their support to the National Party, a change that no observer would have thought possible in the early 1980s.

Seen in the light of long-term historical developments, one should hesitate to describe the dramatic moves of President De Klerk in 1990-93—releasing Mandela, unbanning the ANC and the Communist Party and then scrapping most of the sacred statutes of apartheid—as the defeat and dismantling of apartheid. Perhaps these moves should be seen rather as just another supple manoeuvre, another mystifying change of face designed not to kill off apartheid but to ensure its immortality.

Bennun's article explains how, in spite of the much heralded changes of the early 1990s, apartheid's long-term strategy remained very much intact. The grand design of apartheid had always been to divide the black population by emphasising ethnic divisions and 'tribal' cultures at the expense of the idea of a single black nationalism. The crude attempt to restore the rule of chiefs in 'Bantu' tribal reserves in the 1950s was replaced by a more sophisticated policy which took Britain's High Commission Territories as a model and sought to create tribal homelands which would eventually achieve independence. Such a policy would only succeed if ethnic identity could be made to triumph in African minds over black nationalism, and black nationalists, whether of the ANC, the PAC, Black Consciousness or the Communist persuasion, responded with their universalist ideologies.

It was an essential device of apartheid not just to emphasise ethnic differences, and to seek to promote them through propaganda devices ranging from segregated education to 'tribal' dancing displays in mine compounds, but actually to promote violence within the black community—a violence which would exacerbate ethnic division as people were forced to look to their own ethnic group for protection. It is essential to appreciate that, from the point of view of the Government, it did not much matter what form the violence took—violence by criminal gangs or *tsotsis*, rape and murder in the township streets, shebeen violence, taxi wars or political violence between organised supporters of political or ethnic groups. Any form of violence undermined black unity and promoted ethnic hostilities. Moreover communal violence also had the effect of diverting black people from the struggle against the white apartheid regime. So deeply rooted was this mode of conducting politics that it was used in a quite deliberate way by the NP in the Western Cape during the elections of April 1994. In spite of the show of close co-operation at the top between Mandela and De Klerk, the NP campaign organisers sought to attract coloured votes by putting out the most outrageous anti-black propaganda.

This policy of tolerating violence and promoting ethnicity was implicit in apartheid from the start. When Alan Paton wrote *Cry the Beloved Country* in 1947, black violence in the townships was already perceived by whites as a major issue, but according to Paton it was seen largely as a threat to white security. By the 1950s the Government had taken adequate security measures to protect the white community and was able to let township violence run its course. In an article published in 1976, Nicholas Petryszack pointed out that Soweto had become one of the most violent cities in the world. Murders and rapes went uninvestigated and unreported, and 'twenty murders in Soweto in a single weekend [was] a common occurrence'. Violence within the black community was not something to be deplored by the white rulers of South Africa—it was even something to be promoted. As a form of 'displaced aggression' it was essential to the continuation of white rule.[5]

In this context the emergence of Inkatha is of significance. At first Inkatha was a political movement formed to support Gatsha Buthelezi's power base in the kwaZulu Homeland. However, any uneasiness which whites may have felt at the size and organisation of Inkatha and at the unwillingness of Buthelezi to accept formal independence for kwaZulu, was soon replaced by a perception of the value that this movement had in achieving apartheid's longer-term objectives. Already during the Soweto rising of 1976 Zulu hostel dwellers had shown their hostility to the black insurrectionists, and there followed fifteen years of ever closer co-operation between Inkatha and the Government, with the South African Defence Force (SADF) training the kwaZulu police and secret service funds being channelled to Buthelezi to build up his organisation, found trades unions, and hold rallies. Meanwhile Inkatha gradually developed a political standpoint favourable to the long-term

---

5. Nicholas Petryszack, 'The Dynamics of Acquiescence in South Africa', 1976 *African Affairs* 444-462.

Introduction

apartheid interests. Buthelezi opposed international sanctions and accepted the tenets of white capitalism. More importantly he espoused the cause of federalism or regionalism, an ideology which cleverly updated, but did not radically alter, the old discredited policy of the Homelands. When he was finally dropped by De Klerk in 1993, Buthelezi's conversion to federalism allowed him to form a close political alliance with the extreme right-wing, white Conservative Party.

Seen in this light the violence of the post-1990 period, and the role of Inkatha in it, can be clearly placed in a continuum of policies which have secured apartheid's long-term objectives. It now seems increasingly clear that De Klerk and the National Party realised that the old style of autocratic white rule which had characterised the presidency of P.W. Botha was no longer possible. It had to be replaced with structures that the rest of the world would accept. However, white control of land, labour and political power could still be secured if the black population could be fragmented along ethnic lines, if the marginal groups like Indians and coloureds could be corralled within the white camp, and if a federal constitution could be devised which would, in effect, perpetuate the old Homeland policy under a new guise.

It therefore becomes clear, as Bennun points out, that apparently 'motiveless killings' and 'random violence' are neither random nor motiveless. Some of the violence may be initiated from within Inkatha, PAC or ANC gangs, and some may be carried out by the security forces themselves (for all of which there is abundant evidence) but *any* sort of violence serves the interests of white domination and the long-term strategy of crippling black unity.

However, there is another aspect of the violence which needs to be placed in context. The direct involvement in some of the violence of individual police officers and security units has now been incontrovertibly documented. What, however, is not clear is whether this involvement was part of a conspiracy orchestrated at Cabinet level, or whether it was organised by semi-independent elements within the security forces and merely tolerated by the Cabinet either because ministers dared not interfere or because they secretly saw such insubordination as serving long-term ends. A third explanation is that there has been a deep split within the white camp with sections of the security forces pursuing a separate policy at loggerheads with the government.

That there have been deep divisions within the white nationalist camp ever since the independence of Mozambique and Angola in 1975 is clear. Whereas one policy line was to co-operate with the newly independent states and to secure South Africa's economic hegemony, the other, influenced by Israel's response to the PLO, advocated destabilisation and military attacks on South Africa's neighbours. During the 1980s the policy of destabilisation was pursued although there is doubt about what its ultimate objectives really were. Although it was ostensibly aimed at ANC bases and offices abroad, this was only the excuse for what appears to have been a deeper strategy. Destabilisation served four, rather ill thought-out but still detectable, objectives. Firstly it aimed to cripple the economies of the `Front-line States', thereby forcing them into dependence on South Africa. Secondly, it was designed to prevent them acting effectively as a united front in regional or world politics. Thirdly, it was designed to win the support of the USA by representing southern Africa as a crucial battlefield in the struggle against world communism. Finally, it was intended to secure South Africa's oil and arms supply routes in case these were seriously threatened by sanctions.

Destabilisation took the form of commando raids, bombings, destruction of railways and economic installations, and attempted mercenary coups in the Seychelles, the Comoros and possibly Sao Tomé. However, the most notorious aspect of destabilisation was the arming, training and supplying of dissident guerrilla groups in neighbouring countries. South African support for UNITA and for RENAMO is well documented. Support for UNITA fitted closely with US policy and with the war being fought against SWAPO in Namibia but it is the RENAMO case which has most bearing on the violence in South Africa itself.

RENAMO was originally formed as a group of black mercenaries to support the white Rhodesian military effort after the fall of the Portuguese regime in Mozambique in 1974-5. With the collapse of the Smith regime, RENAMO's units were transferred to South Africa where they were trained at a camp in northern Transvaal. From there

Introduction

they infiltrated Mozambique to 'destabilise' the Frelimo Government. From the start RENAMO used methods of extreme violence. Although many of its attacks were aimed at key economic installations, its most notorious tactic was to terrorise the civilian population which it did with dramatic and horrific effect. It is now fairly clear that the objective of this terror was to force the population to fragment, to abandon any support for the Government and to find what refuge it could in local 'traditional' communities, religion and even the protection of RENAMO itself. Indiscriminate 'motiveless' and 'random' violence was used as a political weapon to undermine the principal objective of a black nationalist government—the building of national unity on a non-ethnic base.[6]

In 1984 at Nkomati the South African Government signed a peace accord with Frelimo which restored normal relations, in which each party agreed to stop subversive activity against the other and in which South Africa effectively recognised the Frelimo Government. In the light of subsequent events the unbanning of the ANC can be seen as a wholly analogous move. The South African Government formally recognised an enemy and legitimised a leadership which it had previously denounced. However, in the case of Mozambique this recognition did not stop the RENAMO activities. Indeed the SADF continued to supply RENAMO and RENAMO intensified its raiding.

There has been some debate about whether the SADF was taking an independent line from that of the South Africa Foreign Affairs Department, but subsequent events have shown that the white regime in South Africa gained most when it has pursued the objectives of apartheid under cover of accepting the liberal, western view of the conduct of national and international affairs. To continue the subversion of Mozambique while formally recognising and even providing aid to its government is perfectly in accord with the subsequent policy of ruthlessly trying to destabilise the ANC while outwardly recognising its existence and negotiating in a cordial manner with its leaders.

Mervyn Bennun's chapter, therefore, analyses the post-1990 violence in terms of direct government involvement, the secret activities of security agencies, and the long-term white objectives

---

6. For a detailed study of RENAMO see Vines, A., *RENAMO: Terrorism in Mozambique* (Currey, London) 1991; and Wilson, K.B., n. 2, above.

which are served by communal violence. However, the main thrust of his conclusion, is that apartheid is far from dead and that the policies pursued by President De Klerk's Government between 1990 and April 1994 were all deeply rooted in the 'classic' apartheid period.

2 CONSTITUTION-MAKING

It is against the background of violence, and the strong possibility that there is a hidden agenda which seeks the continuation and not the end of apartheid, that the constitutional talks are being pursued. South Africa has a long history of constitution-making: the laws of the Dutch East India Company were followed by the granting of a colonial assembly to the Cape by the British; in 1853 the Cape was granted representative government, and Natal received its first constitution in 1856. The 'trekker' republics established their fundamental laws between 1854 and 1858. In 1872 the Cape was granted yet another constitution conferring responsible government status and between 1874 and 1880 the British Government tried to form a Confederation of the white states in southern Africa. The constitutional powers of the South African Republic (Transvaal) were redefined in 1882 and 1884 at the Pretoria and London Conventions. Meanwhile Queen Adelaide Province, British Kaffraria, Griqualand West and British Bechuanaland came and went, all being eventually absorbed by the growing Cape Colony. Basutoland was joined to the Cape in 1871 but became a British protectorate in 1884, while the Transkei was finally brought under Cape administration in 1894 with a special constitutional status. In 1893 Natal was granted responsible government and in 1902, after the South African War, the Transvaal and the Orange Free State became Crown Colonies and an attempt was made to alter the constitution of the Cape.

With scarcely a lull constitution-making resumed. The Transvaal received self-government in 1906 and the OFS in 1907, while Swaziland was finally hived off from the Transvaal and became a protectorate in 1907. In 1908, after many inter-colonial conferences, a constitutional convention was held which led to the British Parliament passing the Act which established the Union of South Africa in 1910. This constitution was to last until 1983 but not without major

Introduction

modifications. In 1919 German South West Africa was given to the Union as a mandate of the League of Nations and in 1923 the British Government tried unsuccessfully to make Southern Rhodesia join the Union. In 1926 Hertzog published his Four Bills which finally resulted in the first major alteration of the constitution in 1936. Shortly after achieving power in 1948 the National Party altered the constitution by allowing the whites in South West Africa to elect members to the Union parliament, by introducing major constitutional changes to remove the last voting rights of non-whites in the Cape which was eventually passed in 1956, and finally by holding a referendum to establish a Republic in 1961. Meanwhile the elaboration of emergency security legislation in fact modified the constitution still further by fundamentally altering the balance of power in the state in favour of the executive, while the Homeland legislation was also designed to undo the work of 1910 and to break up the South African Union. Finally a wholly new constitution, which was first mooted in 1977 and came into effect in 1983, replaced the old 'Westminster' style constitution with a presidential government supported by a tricameral legislature based on ethnic distinctions.

Constitution-making is therefore nothing new in South Africa and it is important to see the negotiations of the early 1990s in a historical context, as many of the issues that complicated the negotiations have historical precedents.

At all periods constitution-makers in South Africa have had to try to reconcile sharply divergent communal and class interests and rivalries. In addition their work has always had to take account of the pressures stemming from black African societies inside and outside the borders, and from superpower interests (Britain and Germany in the nineteenth century, US and USSR in the twentieth). The nineteenth century constitutions in Cape Colony created a working alliance between British imperial interests and wealthy Afrikaner landowners. It was achieved through the device of a franchise limited by property and education qualifications that included some blacks and coloureds and excluded some Afrikaners. This was the origin of the famous 'Cape Liberalism' defended in the twentieth century by many politicians of Afrikaner as well as British origin. It was a liberalism that, under the pretence of establishing civil rights for all, in fact guaranteed the power of the land-owning class. This constitutional balance was threatened, first by the growing wealth of the black population and then by the growing poverty of the 'poor white' Afrikaners. The black threat was avoided by the creation of a special status for the populous Transkei region. The Transkei was excluded from the provisions of the Cape franchise and given its own 'tribal' government in the Bunga—the beginnings of the Homeland policy. Basutoland was also hived off from the Cape in 1884 after an unhappy twelve years of Cape rule and a Homeland type of constitution was created there as well under the king and the Pitso (the Sotho assembly).

The story of the Cape constitution is therefore one where a limited franchise guaranteed white power while granting civil rights to a minority of coloureds and blacks, and dealing with the mass of the black population by establishing Homelands ruled by 'tribal' institutions under white tutelage.

The 'poor white threat' manifested itself chiefly in the former Republics and became the major concern of constitution-makers in the early twentieth century who saw the communal, ethnic rivalry of English and Afrikaner as the principal threat to the idea of a united South Africa. The British predilection for a Cape-style constitution was opposed by the Afrikaner politicians who saw that the only way to counter imperial dominance was to mobilise the Afrikaner 'masses' When universal male suffrage for whites was conceded, the issue turned on the delicate question of whether constituency boundaries would be drawn to have equal numbers of voters or equal numbers of white population. Equal numbers of voters would have given the British element in the Transvaal voting dominance as there were thought to be more English than Afrikaner males in the population. But constituencies based on population size (that is males, females and children) would swing the electoral advantage in favour of Afrikaners.

In spite of the Transvaal being given a constitution which the British thought would ensure an 'English' electoral victory, the Afrikaner *Het Volk* won the first Transvaal elections having succeeded in winning over some of the English vote and splitting the rest. Milner, Jameson and the pro-imperial party had played communal politics and had prompted a nationalist, and in the Orange River Colony a republican, response among the Afrikaners. However, after the 1907 elections in

Introduction

the Transvaal power was held by a party which represented a coalition of interests and drew support from both communities. Ethnic hatchets were soon buried and in the 1907 Rand miners strike, the former Boer generals called on the imperial government to use British troops in support of the mine owners to crush a strike among white miners, some of whom were of Afrikaner origin. Class interest and ethnic identity were already weaving a pattern of some complexity in South African politics.

The forming of the 1910 constitution is of great interest in throwing light on the negotiations of the 1990s. Union was wanted by the imperial government, by the mine owners, and by both moderate and extreme Afrikaner nationalists. All these factions, though deeply opposed to each other, thought that Union would serve their interests and rapidly resolved their disagreement over the details of the constitution. The opponents of Union, the handful of Transvaal separatists, Natal, the advocates of a federation and the black and coloured population, found no basis for unity among themselves. There was no alliance of convenience such as emerged in 1993 between Buthelezi and the extreme Afrikaner right wing.

The constitution was drawn up not by a democratically elected assembly but by representatives of the colonial governments meeting as a convention. The major issues which were hotly debated, and any one of which could have wrecked the negotiations, are arrestingly familiar to those following South African affairs in the 1990s: federalism versus the unitary state; enfranchisement of the black population; the inclusion or exclusion of the Protectorates (the Homelands of the day); and the entrenching of certain constitutional rights (a Bill of Rights). The outcome of these debates is worth recalling.

The Union constitution produced a unitary state but with a marked federal character. There were two capitals (with Bloemfontein, where the Supreme Court sat, effectively a third) and very strong provincial governments which, for example, controlled education. The historic divisions of colony and republic became the new provinces. The qualified franchise was retained in the Cape with its theoretical possibility of mass black enfranchisement, but this franchise was not extended to the rest of South Africa—another significant federal aspect of the 1910 constitution; the 'Homelands' were not constitutionally incorporated—the Transkei retained its separate status within Cape

Province and the three Protectorates, although economically integrated through a customs union, remained under imperial rule. As for entrenching constitutional rights—the equality of the English and Dutch languages was given special protected status as was the Cape franchise, which the law courts soon interpreted as meaning the right of all people in the Cape to acquire and own land.

The 1910 Union constitution proved very difficult to alter. The infringement of African rights in the 1913 Land Act was ruled to be unconstitutional; the exclusion of the Protectorates became permanent despite sustained efforts by successive South African governments to have them incorporated in the Union; and the ending of black and coloured voting rights in the Cape took from 1926 to 1956 to achieve. The difficulties which successive governments encountered in their attempts to amend or repeal the entrenched clauses shows just how effective a 'Bill of Rights' can become.

The outcome of the Union constitution in terms of power structures is also of interest. Neither of the competing ethnic groups, the 'imperial' English and nationalist Afrikaners, were able to win control of the Union Government. Until 1948 all governments in South Africa held power only with substantial support from both communities, either through formal coalitions like the Pact Government of 1924 or in the informal coalitions of interests that led to the creation of the South African Party and then the United Party. In 1948 the Union Government was captured by a coalition of extreme Afrikaner parties but two observations are pertinent. Firstly, the NP of Malan, Strijdom and Verwoerd failed to win a hundred per cent Afrikaner support, and it is estimated that at least fifteen to twenty per cent of Afrikaners continued to vote against it at elections even at the height of its power in the 1960s. Secondly, by the early 1960s Verwoerd had begun the policy of wooing English votes and turning the NP, like other South African ruling parties before it, into a coalition drawing on English, Afrikaner and, after 1974, on Portuguese support.

It is no surprise to find that issues similar to those which historically have preoccupied South African politicians were debated in the CODESA forum in its attempt to act as midwife to a new constitutional order in the 1990s. The issues in this debate are explored in the chapter by Nico Steytler. The most contentious issue of all proved to be

Introduction

deciding which body would draw up the new constitution. In 1910 the constitution had been devised by a convention made up of representatives of the self-governing colonies and enacted by the British Parliament. In 1983 it was the white South African Parliament which then legitimised its decisions in a referendum. In the 1990s it became a question of whether the constitution would be drawn up by representatives of the various political groups that made up CODESA, or whether there would first be elections for a constituent assembly which would draw up the constitution—the solution which was eventually agreed.

The issues need to be starkly revealed for what they are. In CODESA a large number of political parties and groups were represented but the formal equality they had in the CODESA discussions did not reflect the level of support they might win in an election to a constituent assembly. In particular the extreme right-wing white groups, Inkatha and the PAC feared with some justification that they would win so little support in an election that they would lose any effective voice in making the constitution. The ANC remained confident of its massive popular appeal throughout and the NP played a canny game. Knowing that it was the only serious rival to the ANC and was in a position to pick up the support of many minorities and marginal groups, it first took up a position that it wanted the constitution decided before elections. However, as its support grew it increasingly conceded the ANC's position since it saw that it had a realistic expectation of being influential if not dominant in a constituent assembly.

The same calculations have surrounded the issue of whether the citizens of the four Homelands which have been granted formal independence (Bophutatswana, Venda, Ciskei and Transkei) should vote. The Homeland leaders have been fearful of losing their leverage on South African affairs and the NP wanted, if possible, to limit the size of the popular vote for the ANC. In 1910 the chiefs of the Protectorates were also anxious to be omitted from the constitution of the Union while the white politicians wanted to include the Protectorates and the Transkeian territories, but only on condition that they would be denied access to civil rights and the vote. In the end the British Government decided that the Protectorates would be left out of the Union, partly to provide themselves with a bargaining position to ensure the good behaviour of the South Africa Government in the future and partly to safeguard black rights at least in part of southern Africa when it was sacrificing these rights elsewhere.

As in 1910 a great deal of the constitutional debate has revolved around the issue of whether the new South Africa would have a federal or a unitary structure. Clearly some minority groups envisage a break up of South Africa into a number of small states—an Afrikaner state, a Zulu state, a Tswana state, a Xhosa state, etc. Around this concept was built, during the middle of 1993, an overt alliance between extreme right-wing white groups, Inkatha and some of the Homeland leaders. This political development made explicit the linkages that had always existed between Inkatha and right-wing elements in the white community. It also showed once again to what extent apartheid, the legacy of Verwoerd, lived on. The old Homeland policy, so discredited in the 1980s and effectively abandoned by the Government as unworkable, was to be revived under the guise of federalism.

The ANC has been determined to resist the fragmentation of South Africa if at all possible but the NP has kept its options open, opposing the break up of South Africa but supporting, as in 1910, the idea of a constitution with a strong federal flavour to it. The history of South Africa suggests that the two ideals can be combined as they were in the 1910 constitution: strong regional or ethnic identities can be reconciled with the idea of a unitary, multi-ethnic state. However, to achieve this in a world which has witnessed ethnic cleansing and the partition of Bosnia, not to mention the cynical arming of UNITA to create mayhem within Angola, must be an extraordinarily, almost impossibly, difficult task unless the international community backs the process with a resolution it has not shown elsewhere.

Important also were the discussions over the control of the media, the security forces and the conduct of the election itself. These discussions show how much the participants have learnt from the recent history of elections in Africa. The importance of Britain's participation in the Rhodesian independence elections is clear, as was Britain's unequivocal acceptance of the results. Equally important was the role the international community played in the independence of Namibia. A new South African constitution will almost certainly also require some

Introduction

international assistance before it can come into being. As Steytler argues, there might be a role for international agencies in providing logistical support for the election process itself—monitors, security personnel, election officials—but the principal contribution that outsiders can make will be to monitor the elections fairly, to recognise the victors and to discountenance those who might seek to overturn the verdict of the ballot box, whoever they may be. The Angolan elections of 1992 are a crucial warning. Here the Government allowed itself to be disarmed and to hold elections under UN auspices, only to find that the rest of the world did not support it when it won the elections, and its rivals, who had not disarmed, refused to accept the result and restarted the fighting. While the Angolan crisis continues, a threat must hang over a democratic future for South Africa. If those who lose elections, judged fair by the UN, can then resort to arms with the expectation of being given support by elements of the international community, then the whole democratic process is fatally flawed.

3 THE ROLE OF LAW AND LEGAL INSTITUTIONS

While it is clearly important to analyse developments in South Africa in terms of the different interest groups and their struggle for a say in the future, the main objective of this book is to suggest that law, legal institutions and legal processes should provide the backbone of any political structure that may emerge. The efficiency of a regime, and the quality of life it can offer to the people of a country, are immeasurably improved if flexible and efficient legal frameworks and institutions are in place to assist it. It is a commonplace that governments can benefit by having the backing of courts to enforce the law, but it is less often appreciated that social stability itself can be fundamentally improved if the law is seen to be both even handed in its operation and willing and able to protect individuals and minorities.

Many people have attached great significance to the role that a Bill of Rights might play in a future South Africa. It is assumed that in a pluralistic society a Bill of Rights, or some similar constitutional device, can provide a real measure of protection to minorities against majority tyranny. There is an old constitutional debate about whether the powers of the legislature are absolute. In England the supremacy of statute law over custom, common law, natural law and church law was firmly established at the time of the Reformation—indeed it can be said to have been finally settled with the beheading of Sir Thomas More in 1528. Since then, those attempting to protect property or to promote religious freedom or civil rights have always sought to do so through statute law. The only major example in England of the use of the courts rather than Parliament to establish constitutional rights was the 1772 Mansfield judgment which declared slavery to be unlawful.

However, many countries have sought in written constitutions, concordats, or declarations of rights a way to limit the supremacy of statute law—or more precisely to make it impossible for the weapon of statute law to be employed by a simple majority acting on a single occasion to destroy civil and constitutional rights. There are a number of different ways that a Bill of Rights, or entrenched clauses in a constitution, can define a citizen's rights. There can be general principles—like freedom of speech, freedom of assembly, freedom of worship or, vaguer still, 'life, liberty and the pursuit of happiness'—or there can be specific and precisely defined rights like the entrenching of the provisions of the Cape constitution in the Act of Union or the declaration of the equal status of two languages. However, some constitutions have also included 'directive principles' which enshrine sets of socio-economic objectives. Those in the first category are sometimes described as 'enforceable' or 'first generation' rights. They are enforceable in a negative sense, in that the courts can intervene in a negative way to declare legislation that contravenes such rights to be illegal. The 'directive principles' are referred to as 'non-enforceable' or 'second generation' rights. These, it is argued, need positive state action if they are to be realised.

These issues are discussed by Pierre de Vos who looks at the way these two different concepts of rights were handled in the Indian constitution and how the courts have subsequently treated them, and by Andrew Caiger who examines the specific, and highly contentious, example of property rights.

When the Indian constitution was drawn up in 1949, it included a section, Part III, which listed certain 'fundamental rights' which included basic civil rights such as freedom of speech and assembly. It was stated that no statute would be lawful if it infringed these rights,

Introduction

but at the same time it made provision for them to be changed by making it possible for alterations to be made to the constitution itself. These rights could be exercised either by cases being brought before the supreme court to be tested or by judicial review. In another part of the constitution, Part IV, certain 'unenforceable directive principles' were set out which included social and economic objectives. It became the business of constitutional lawyers for the next forty years to decide how to reconcile the two parts of the constitution—how to proceed when measures taken to realise the 'directive principles' (the policy objectives in Part IV) ran counter to the fundamental rights set out in Part III.

This is one of the oldest and most fundamental of constitutional dilemmas. On the one hand the community as a whole, embodied in the legislative organs of the state, must have the power to pursue its objectives and make laws to suit its needs, and the constitutional principle that no legislative assembly can bind its successors must retain validity. On the other hand individuals must be able to look to the law to protect their rights and interests not only against other members of the community but also against the arbitrary power of the government of the day.

Pierre de Vos' conclusions are that Indian constitutional lawyers, in testing the validity of the rights established in the constitution, fully explored this dilemma, veering from one interpretation to another before finally settling on a single line of argument. The line eventually adopted, however, has great significance for the future constitution of South Africa. It is that there is no 'conceptual difference—or any difference in status' between fundamental 'first generation' rights and so-called 'second generation' rights such as the 'directive principles' of the Indian constitution. The latter can be enforced by the courts and a supreme court would have the power not only to declare invalid legislation which, for example, contravened freedom of speech or freedom of assembly, but would also be able to review *all* legislation in the light of the 'directive principles' (the so-called 'non-enforceable' rights) to see if it contravened the declared objectives of the constitution. In India, as de Vos says, 'the directive principles assist the court in determining where the boundaries of the fundamental rights should be set, whether restrictions on fundamental rights by the legislator or the executive are reasonable.' This has meant that the courts have taken an active as opposed to a purely passive role in the political process, although it was thirty years before the supreme court was able 'to unlock the potential of the directive principles'.

The importance of this for South Africa is considerable. It has been suggested, not least by the ANC, that a new South African constitution should contain both fundamental rights and non-enforceable directive principles. Whereas individuals and minorities would be able look to a statement of 'fundamental rights', enshrined in the constitution, for protection against arbitrary state action, the majority would be able to find in the 'directive principles' affirmations of its social and economic objectives which the courts would also be prepared to uphold. However, De Vos points out that courts should not be called on to make policy. 'It would be dangerous...merely to include all social and economic rights as a "shopping list" in a Bill of Rights with the vague hope that the judiciary would stir the pot and come up with innovative enforcement mechanisms.' Moreover he stresses the need for the constitution to include only rights that 'can be formulated with precision' and which have been 'agreed on beforehand would be affordable and within reach of the national budget.'

The prior history of South Africa indicates that rights entrenched in a formal constitution are very difficult indeed to alter. Although the Act of Union gave political power unequivocally to the white population, the final removal of the constitutional rights for blacks and coloureds in the Cape proved a laborious and prolonged process. Moreover in the litigation that followed the 1913 Land Act the South African courts extended the scope of the entrenched clauses into a form of protection of property rights for non-whites in the Cape.

This latter aspect of the constitution of 1910, the right to property, remerges as a matter of fundamental concern in the formation of the 1990s constitution. Ownership of property, and in particular ownership of land, has been identified as an issue of contention that could wreck a constitutional settlement. As Andrew Caiger points out, 'land exercises a special force in the psyche of South Africans' and has become a symbol of community identity. Many Africans still seek or enjoy customary rights to land as members of a community while ownership of land certainly constitutes one of the factors by which Afrikaner communities define their identity. The Land Acts of 1913 and 1936,

Introduction

the Group Areas Act of 1950 and the removals of population consequent upon these Acts, are some of the aspects of apartheid perceived by blacks as most pernicious, while they are seen by some whites as having established their rights to property. A majority government will certainly seek a land redistribution while minority communities will equally certainly look to a Bill of Rights to protect property ownership.

The chapters by Caiger and De Vos make clear the inevitable limitations on what a Bill of Rights can and should seek to achieve. In the cases of Kenya, Zambia, Malawi and Zimbabwe the constitutions were changed to remove the safeguards that had been put into them at the time of independence, and there is no way in which a South African Bill of Rights or the articles of a new constitution can preserve for all time individual rights to individual pieces of property. What, however, they should seek to do is to prevent arbitrary confiscation and, through judicial review, ensure that any compulsory purchase is in accordance with a reasonable interpretation of the aims of the constitution which may be set out, as in the Indian constitution, as a series of 'directive principles'. So much can be seen as a legitimate protection for property rights, but a Bill of Rights, as De Vos points out, should enable the courts to be active in actually promoting measures to ensure the realisation of the aims of the constitution. In India the courts extended their interpretative role to 'discovering' new rights implicit in those which were actually spelt out in the constitution. Thus they discovered in the 'right to life' a new constitutional 'right to a livelihood'. In this way radical opinion in South Africa could see a Bill of Rights, not as a buttress of the status quo but as an active force for realising change.

However, the issue of property rights is far more complex than merely defining and guaranteeing the ownership of the freehold on land. In the parts of South Africa where whites acquired freehold rights to land, Africans were often allowed, or even encouraged, to continue to live on the land as squatters or as tenants 'farming on the half'. Indeed a wide variety of quasi-customary arrangements came into existence to reconcile the interests of landowners and squatters. Numerous pieces of legislation, the Land Act of 1913 being merely the best known of them, tried to deal with squatting; but the changing needs of white farmers for labour and of Africans for land, and the changing relative values of these commodities in the marketplace meant that squatting survived all the legal prohibitions of different governments. More recently the intolerable pressures of urbanisation bursting the straitjacket of apartheid laws has led to the development of 'squatter' townships and to the establishment of new communities on unoccupied state, municipal and private land.

The concept of property rights has, therefore, to take into account the rights of land use which are enshrined in custom or are merely being claimed *de facto*. As Caiger shows, the De Klerk Government was ill equipped both politically and legally to cope with the problems posed by squatting. The law allowed different courses of action which the Government pursued according to the strength of the different interest groups in each particular case. However, the courts have already, through their judgments, strengthened the position of squatters and—

> ...have held on two separate occasions that there is an obligation on the local authority to consider what is to become of the squatters... In these cases the squatters have usually gained permission for a temporary sojourn and once permission has been given it becomes more difficult to remove them.

Pressures on space can certainly be one of the most important conditions in which communal violence flares up and it is a field where the law can play a mediating and pacifying role. However, the task of reconciling the idea of freehold right to land, with all that that implies in terms of providing collateral, with the African traditions of access to and use of land, is formidable and cannot easily be tackled by a few high-sounding phrases in a Bill of Rights. The precedent exists for shared access to land, as Caiger says, and the concept of property rights has to encompass more than just freehold. 'The "right" a person has in property will be determined within a context of community values'. Perhaps the traditions of Roman Law which recognised different types of title to property can be reinvoked to find a solution.

The issue remains to be resolved in the constitution that will be produced between 1994 and 1999. In the meantime the transitional constitution declares that any person or community can claim restitution of land of which they were deprived in a racially

Introduction

discriminatory manner at any time since 1913. A commission will draw up a report on claims that will be submitted to legal process—a formula which at first sight seems to offer little to claimants and leaves everything to the way the courts interpret their role.

4 MEDIATING PEACE

Competition for land and living space is merely one major cause of communal conflict, and commentators looking at the violence in South Africa have found many others. Unemployment and competition for jobs, rivalry between bus and taxi operators, conditions in the hostels, even the new gender and generation relationships within the shanty townships all appear as factors which have led to conflict. These generalised and unfocused concerns are sharpened by ideology or party rivalry into the violent clashes that have turned many of the townships into a sort of battlefield. Although there is no ultimate solution to the underlying causes of conflict except through political action, the law and legal institutions can significantly help in dealing with the immediate causes of individual incidents and so help to untwist the spiral of violence.

It is a truism that where a community has no recourse to the law or to the police, opportunities abound for vigilantes, criminal gangs, warlords, etc., to fill the vacuum. However, in South Africa the police itself has been a partisan instrument of state oppression and the courts have seldom offered the ordinary black or coloured person the opportunity for redress. The important revelations of the collusion between the State and Inkatha and of the clandestine activities of elements of the security forces have made the creation of lawkeeping institutions which can be trusted by all communities of the utmost importance. The National Peace Accord which was signed on 14 September 1991 and the subsequent Internal Peace Institutions Act passed in June 1992 are, therefore, major landmarks in the creation of a post-apartheid South Africa. This statement is made advisedly and in the full knowledge that the Peace Accord did not lead to an immediate improvement in communal relations. Indeed the months following the signing saw an escalation of violence and a deepening of the social crisis. However, as J.R. Midgley writes, 'the Act was the first product of multilateral negotiations to be enacted as law and even though it was passed by an unrepresentative Parliament, it was the first statute which purported to reflect the considered opinions of a substantial portion of disenfranchised South Africans'. It put in place what were potentially the first major post-apartheid civil institutions—the first civil institutions to which Africans contributed and to which they genuinely had access.

The National Peace Accord established three important public institutions: the National Peace Committee, the National Peace Secretariat and the Commission of Inquiry into the Prevention of Public Violence, better known as the Goldstone Commission. The National Peace Committee immediately became involved in two aspects of public life which will be decisive in the development of post-apartheid South Africa. It began the official monitoring of the police and the South African Defence Force (SADF) and it began work to coordinate the raising of funds for community projects, concentrating on 'projects that would facilitate peace and defuse violence'. The Goldstone Commission, not studied in any detail in this book, rapidly acquired a reputation for vigour and impartiality and its numerous reports on the background to violence went a long way towards establishing some credibility for public institutions in a situation that might have deteriorated rapidly towards civil war. As Midgley writes, 'monitoring remains one of the more important tasks of the peace structures. It has a specific complementary role in the pursuit of peace. In placing the behaviour of people under the spotlight, monitoring encourages self-discipline.'

It is the National Peace Secretariat and the 'peace committees' that it set up which are the principal object of Midgley's study. Regional and Local Peace Committees came into existence so that 'disputes should be settled by using simple and expeditious procedures' through the intervention of official mediators or 'facilitators'. The Peace Committees were 'to gain their legitimacy by representing the people and the communities they are designed to serve' but Midgley's chapter shows how the Government of De Klerk tried to capture the institutions of the Peace Accord in order to retain ultimate control over the appointment of personnel and over the general operation of its provisions. He quotes John Lamola of the South African Council of Churches who pointed out that the Government had been made 'the

Introduction

guardian and guarantor of the Peace Accord...the virtual patron and commander-in-chief of the National Peace Accord and its structures.' The system of management and accountability made them 'in theory at least accountable...to the Minister of Justice and the State President'. In this way what had been planned to be genuine community action threatened to 'become the eyes and ears of the security forces'.

This may seem to be yet a further indication that apartheid is not dead, that the present turmoil is in fact merely a transformation out of which a new apartheid will eventually emerge, but it presents also a further indication of the process of change that is at work in the South African revolution—the old racist centralism of the NP is in a state of dialectic with the ideology of populist democracy and with the urgent demands of the situation in the townships which calls for flexibility and pragmatism. As Midgley writes,

> It is often said that participation in Peace Committees allows for interaction with opponents without anyone losing political credibility. The peace process has introduced multiparty engagement and political accountability at a local level, and is preparing societies for a democracy.

The determination of so many people to make the Peace Accord, and the institutions it set up, a working reality presents a kind of dress rehearsal for the way a new compromise constitution for South Africa may have to operate in the future.

Chapter Two

Understanding the Nightmare: Politics and Violence in South Africa

Mervyn E. Bennun

1 INTRODUCTION

The nature of the violence currently rampant in South African society needs to be examined in a political context if it is to be understood. This chapter is an attempt to make such an examination, using an elementary categorisation of the violence, and to point to some of its implications. The categories overlap, the categorisation as a whole may be thought to be somewhat rough and ready, and the conclusions broad; but it is suggested that the broad picture is defensible because it explains otherwise puzzling behaviour.

No apology is offered for the relative absence of officially-published statistical material. The reason for this is well put by Simpson and Rauch:[1]

> Official crime statistics are notoriously unreliable. In particular, police statistics reflect only reported incidents. In cases of political violence where police are perceived to be partisan, the reporting rates are probably drastically skewed.

Moreover, until the allegations of misconduct and responsibility against the police and army have been resolved it is difficult to trust any statistical information they are responsible for.

---

1. Simpson, G. and Rauch, J. 'Review of Violence 1991', Project for the study of violence, Psychology Department, University of the Witwatersrand.

Understanding the Nightmare: Politics and Violence in South Africa

Various independent unofficial agencies in South Africa have made an effort to compile information. The Human Rights Commission in particular publishes a weekly *Repression Report* and monthly *Area Repression Reports*:[2]

> These reports are drawn up by HRC researchers located in Johannesburg, Durban, Cape Town and Port Elizabeth, from information culled from the Press, electronic media, police unrest reports, community organisations, church groups, trade unions, political organisations, monitoring groups, and others. In each incident reported the source references are quoted.

One claim made by the HRC should be noted: it maintains that its figures 'are compiled on the arbitrary premise that any incident in which ten or more people died should be classified as a massacre'. In view of the prevailing conditions it seems highly unlikely that any more reliable basis for such figures will ever emerge. Any distortion in the data compiled from these sources certainly cannot be attributed to a want of objectivity on the part of the HRC; one should however bear in mind, in view of what follows below, that the editorial policy of the daily press is not generally characterised by sympathy for the African National Congress and the organisations associated with it.

Some figures, however, are worth noting. According to one account, there was a total of 11,764 murders committed between January and August 1991; of these, 4.62 per cent were solved by the police and an offender faced a less than 10 per cent chance of prosecution.[3] There is no agreement on how many of these deaths are politically related: during the period referred to, the police claimed that 806 were related to unrest or political violence, while the Human Rights Commission put the figure at 1,161.[4] Eighty-one deaths are attributed to the police—presumably these are deaths which the police

---

2. Coleman, M. (1992) *Political Violence in South Africa: an Overview of Two Years of Destabilisation July 1990 to June 1992*. Human Rights Commission: Johannesburg.
3. *Weekly Mail*, 22 - 28 November 1992.
4. The figures are derived from tables prepared by the Human Rights Commission, *Statistical Summary: an Overview of Two Years of Destabilisation—July 1990 to June 1992*, Appendix 1, Figure 1.

acknowledge that they were responsible for, and not cases where they are alleged to have been responsible. It appears also that these were all politically-related cases.

The Commonwealth Observer Mission to South Africa made an attempt, at the beginning of 1993, to describe the incidence of violent crime. It reported that the South African Police recorded 14,693 murders in South Africa in 1991 and that the figures for 1992 were expected to exceed 15,000.[5] The Mission also noted the HRC's statement that there would be a total of 3,600 politically motivated deaths in 1992—an average of 10 per day for the year and a rise of more than 40 per cent over 1991.

The HRC recorded 3,689 deaths related to political violence between March 1992 and March 1993. The total for March 1993 alone was 181—a 32 per cent decrease being recorded for the first quarter of 1993 over the corresponding period in 1992.

In the HRC review covering the six months from January to June 1993, issued together with its Monthly Repression Report for June, it is calculated that up to the date of the summary the monthly average for 1993 was 231.2 deaths from political violence, with a total for the period of 1,387 deaths and 2,331 injuries. On 5 August, an ANC official claimed that the figures exceeded those caused by the war in Bosnia-Herzogovnia and the fighting between Serb and Croat forces around Sarajevo.[6] On the East Rand alone, it was claimed that there were more than 700 deaths in July.[7]

2 DESCRIBING THE VIOLENCE

If one depicts the violence in terms which treat all that is happening as part of an undifferentiated whole, it is possible to attribute the killings to racial characteristics and ethnic disputes, so justifying the continued existence of apartheid. On the other hand, if the violence is seen as having a dynamic relationship to the processes of change in South Africa then very different insights into its origins emerge.

---

5. Commonwealth Observer Mission to South Africa, Report: Violence in South Africa. Phase 1: October 1992 - January 1993, Commonwealth Secretariat, London.
6. BBC 'World at One', 5 August, 1993; interview with Carl Niehaus.
7. BBC, 'News at Six', 5 August, 1993.

Thus, for example, addressing the United Nations Security Council in July 1992[8] the South African Minister of Foreign Affairs under the former De Klerk Government ('Pik' Botha) said:

> In the days of apartheid, a variety of differing political groups were united in their opposition to the policies of the day. Now that apartheid has gone, they are no longer united. Their historical, natural differences have come to the fore; differences which among other things, include both ideological and ethnic differences.

This, he explained, was where the causes of the violence lay. He made it clear that it would delay the 'transformation process' involved in abolishing apartheid. Similarly, State President F.W. De Klerk himself claimed on numerous occasions that ethnic rivalry underlay the conflict between the African National Congress and Inkatha; and Gatsha Buthelezi, the President of Inkatha, normally depicted the role of Inkatha as defending Zulu interests against others who sought to belittle them.

The daily press generally resorted to the same analysis. Rupert Taylor, in a helpful study of the causes and ethnic implications of the violence, wrote:[9]

> Media reports linked Zulus with Inkatha, Xhosas with the African National Congress and identified the 'victims' not by their personal names but by ethnic labels, which were taken to determine who lived and who died. Similarly, photographs, especially of crowds, were given ethnic captions.

He draws attention to the editorial position of the *Star*, a Johannesburg paper which he describes as South Africa's most popular, and its description of the conflict as 'tribal warfare' and as 'wild and undirected savagery'. He continues:

---

8. South Africa Communications Services Press Release, *Statement by the South African Minister of Foreign Affairs, Mr. 'Pik' Botha, in the UN Security Council, 16 July 1992.*
9. Rupert Taylor, 'The myth of ethnic division: township conflict on the Reef', *Race and Class*, 33,2 (1991).

With little exception, the media coverage took the ethnic Zulu-Xhosa dimension as a given, in which blame was apportioned equally or not at all; and where in-depth analysis was rejected for a sensationalism that reinforced long-standing colonial stereotypes of Africans as primitive, savage, and prone to violence.

If we accept such analyses then we must inevitably conclude that the majority of South Africans are incapable of participating in the processes of a democratic society, for only apartheid can preserve the peace.

By contrast, Simpson and Rauch[10] locate the violence not only in the social tensions and deprivation, but also in the very processes of change. They find no need to resort to explanations based on ethnicity, and remark that these have

> ...tended to mask the role of effective law enforcement as a potential solution to the problems. The police subculture has tended to perpetuate these sorts of explanations and this is, in large part, responsible for police inactivity and inefficiency in pursuing cases involving black victims.

One should add that the police subculture they refer to did not grow in a void but from the heart of the system of apartheid which is now being overthrown. Simpson and Rauch make a further, telling, point about the use of ethnicity: where ethnic orientation correlates with access to material resources, it becomes exploitable for violence. The 'taxi-wars', it is suggested, illustrate this especially clearly. These foci of bitter and bloody fighting centre around the control of routes over which the ubiquitous taxi-buses operate linking the townships and cities, carrying daily commuters between their homes and work. In a typical incident listed by the HRC, a taxi-driver was shot dead by three armed men in central Johannesburg; he was a member of a taxi association and it was thought that the attack was related to a dispute between it and another over routes, licences, and overcrowded taxi ranks.[11]

It is simply not possible here to give an adequate account of this

---

10. Simpson and Rauch, above, note 1.
11. Monthly Repression Report: April 1993, Human Rights Commission, Johannesburg.

tragic strife, an understanding of which will undoubtedly throw a powerful light on the political role of the police, and the influence of local and community organisations and political parties. The Goldstone Commission had the taxi industry's problems on its agenda, and in its Third Interim Report on the topic[12] referred to the 'sad reading' of the long list of victims who are both those involved in the industry and innocent passengers and pedestrians. The report covers issues such as the massive corruption in the administration of the industry and the issue of licences, the social setting of the industry—the poverty of the community, the paucity of transport for a huge population—and numerous other matters. A more recent account of taxi-related violence in Cape Town supplies a clear image of the community's perception of the police as unwilling, unable or incompetent to deal with the seemingly random killings, if not actually acting in complicity.[13] This is a major topic in itself and forms one part of the issues addressed in this chapter.

2.1 Characterising the Political Violence

Whilst avoiding water-tight and comprehensive categories, it is possible to describe certain distinctive patterns that have emerged.

In the first instance, there were the highly specific and targeted attacks against political activists who either opposed the apartheid system or the previous South African Government; or against those who, as political activists, supported the Government or political organisations which aligned themselves with it. The first group consisted principally of the rank and file of the membership, the leaders, and the structures of the African National Congress, the South African Communist Party, the Congress of South African Trades Unions (COSATU) and various other organisations including local civic organisations. The assassination of Chris Hani on 10 April 1993 is an illustration of this type of incident. The second group of victims was made up principally of members of the Inkatha Freedom Party

---

12. Goldstone Commission, 'Third Interim Report on the violence in the taxi and minibus industry', 4 December 1992.
13. *Weekly Mail*, July 9 - July 15, 1993: 'Mourners Shot At In New Cape Taxi Violence'.

(hereafter, called Inkatha or the IFP) led by Gatsha Buthelezi, which maintained close links with the National Party then in power.

The statistics derived as described above by the Human Rights Commission consistently suggest that both the responsibility for and the burden of the violence were unevenly borne between Inkatha on the one hand and the African National Congress and other organisations associated with it on the other. The HRC figures suggest that between July 1990 and June 1992 Inkatha members, supporters, or others were responsible for 34 (69 per cent) massacres, and township residents and African National Congress supporters were responsible for 6 (12 per cent). A further 3 (6 per cent) were carried out by 'vigilantes' which the HRC described as being 'certainly aligned with Inkatha'. The HRC has calculated that, where the political affiliations of victims during the period January-June 1993 could be ascertained, 186 ANC members were killed as compared with 70 Inkatha members; during the month of June, 26 deaths were of ANC members, and 9 were members of Inkatha. While accepting that these figures are regarded by the compilers themselves as incomplete, they are at least consistent with previous patterns. It is important to note that there may be difficulties in determining political affiliations; the relevance of this point is considered below.

Other analyses of massacres show that between July 1990 and June 1992 the victims were township residents in 36 (73 per cent) of the cases; residents specifically identified as African National Congress supporters were additionally victims in 10 (20 per cent). Inkatha members and supporters were victims in 9 (18 per cent).

The damage caused to the African National Congress, its members and supporters, and the organisations allied with it becomes even more striking when those killings which do not amount to a massacre are included. Bringing political assassinations into the accounting, between January 1990 and April 1992 the HRC recorded a total of 119. It observes that:[14]

> Over 100 of these victims are clearly identifiable as belonging to the anti-apartheid camp, either as officials or members of organisations or as family members, friends and associates caught in the firing line.

---

14. Human Rights Commission, Press Statement No. 92/9, 21 May 1992.

Understanding the Nightmare: Politics and Violence in South Africa

The effects in some parts of the country were devastating. The African National Congress disclosed that during 1991 in the Pretoria-Witwatersrand-Vereeniging triangle (broadly, the densely-populated and industrialised area consisting of Johannesburg and the surrounding urban areas) the movement had been almost crippled through the destruction of the middle tier of its leadership and the creation of a reign of terror which prevented people from organising or attending meetings, and even walking in the streets at night.[15] John Carlin[16] describes the violence as having 'wreaked havoc' on the African National Congress's organising ability. According to the HRC's figures, between July 1990 and June 1992 in the 'PWV Triangle' alone there had been 40 massacres in which at least 1,200 people had died, and just under 60 per cent of all politically-related deaths occurred there.

A great deal of the violence, at first sight, appeared to be motiveless and irrational—typically occurring within the townships and squatter camps. This is hinted at in the HRC's distinction between township residents and African National Congress supporters in the figures given above: one might understand why African National Congress members were targeted, but why people of no affiliation? The press reports described organised and pre-planned attacks, often by groups who seemed to have a degree of training, on what appeared to be random victims who were murdered in their homes or in the streets. In many cases the press reports stated that no clear links were claimed or could be established between the victims and any political organisations.

There was no regular one-to-one relationship between the reported affiliations of victims and attackers: there was no certainty that a report would enable one to conclude that it was an attack by people of an allegedly identifiable political or other affiliation on others with a rival affiliation. This was not necessarily due to poor journalism; the news reports typically commented both on the frequently astonishing degree and scale of the violence, and the apparently 'motiveless' or 'irrational' or 'pointless' or 'meaningless' nature of the incident—a judgment based on the apparent lack of any coherent political pattern, however indefensible.

---

15. *Cape Times*, 25 November, 1991.
16. *Independent*, 24 June, 1992.

For example, a weekly paper[17] carried a report of an attack by gunmen on a house in Soweto in which nine people were shot dead by a group who burst into the house and opened fire at random. They were thought by one of the two survivors (the other was her one-year-old child) to be Inkatha supporters from a local hostel. The woman said that she could think of no reason why her home was singled out. It appears from the report that there was no trace of any political links involving those in the house. An African National Congress official blamed Inkatha and the police for the attack; the former denied responsibility, and the latter were reported to be investigating.[18] The same news item reports also that in the same week in Soweto at least seventeen people were killed in random attacks which commenced after an Inkatha rally on the Sunday. The point is, the attack might have *followed* an Inkatha rally but it cannot be assumed that the victims were linked with Inkatha.

Further illustrations of the phenomenon abound. In June 1993, thirteen bodies were found in Sebokeng; eyewitnesses said that the killings were committed at random by gunmen using assault rifles from a cruising car.[19] This was an incident selected from a weekly toll. Subsequently, a news report of violence in the East Rand township of Daveyton talked of 'residents in constant fear of random attacks by unknown assailants'.[20] The Boipatong massacre itself showed the same randomness in the choice of victims.

Despite the ostensibly random quality, incidents often showed a degree of planning and preparation. Simpson and Rauch draw attention to this factor in the context of their consideration of whether a 'third force' was responsible:

> The cruelty and skill with which the attacks are carried out points to a possibility that these assailants are highly trained and do not identify in any way with their victims.

---

17. *South*, 12-18 December, 1991.
18. It is noticeable that there is an almost complete absence of published reports of the outcomes of such investigations, which must by now be many hundred in number.
19. *Guardian*, Monday 28 June, 1993.
20. *Weekly Mail*, July 30 - August 5 1993: ` "Outsiders" turn Daveyton into killing fields'.

Understanding the Nightmare: Politics and Violence in South Africa

In this context they draw attention to a news report that a group of 1,000 Inkatha members were trained by the SADF in Namibia.[21] The Goldstone Commission confirmed that such training took place, that those involved subsequently took part in criminal violence, and that the various police forces which ought to have investigated this failed to do so efficiently or effectively, with consequent 'negative perceptions' being engendered to the effect that the police themselves were involved.[22] Indeed, many of the attacks throughout the country suggest that planning and training lay behind them—if only to ensure that the attackers acted as a skilled and disciplined group and did not cause each other accidental harm. This must have been especially true of attacks on passengers in the crowded conditions on trains. In one incident near Johannesburg it was reported that the attackers had boarded the train with their weapons hidden in umbrellas, thus evading detection.[23]

Attacks on train passengers are in fact one of the most important manifestations of the violence being considered. According to one study, between July 1990 and April 1992 approximately 200 people were murdered and over 750 injured by groups of attackers using 'traditional weapons' and firearms.[24] In January 1992 a special commission under the auspices of the Goldstone Commission was set up to probe train killings.

In train attacks and others, witnesses and survivors described the assailants as appearing in groups (ten, twenty, and more were not uncommon); of often using police or army vehicles; and of using a variety of firearms and other weapons including grenades. The attackers were often said to have been wearing similar garb or similar disguises and the onslaughts, judging by the press reports, seemed to have the precision of an attack by trained and disciplined men.

The massacre at Boipatong is an example of such an event, although one that was particularly well-publicised, especially abroad. The

---

21. Simpson and Rauch, above, note 1.
22. Goldstone Commission (Commission of inquiry regarding the prevention of public violence and intimidation), Judge Richard Goldstone (chair); 'Allegations concerning front companies of the SADF and the training by the SADF of Inkatha supporters at the Caprivi in 1986', 1 June 1993.
23. *Cape Times*, 19 November, 1991.
24. Memorandum *Violence on Rail Commuters*, prepared by Cheadle Thompson and Haysom, Attorneys, Johannesburg; see, for a fuller account, *Blood on the Tracks: a Special Report on Train Attacks* (1992), Independent Board of

Negotiating Justice

Boipatong reports generally leave in some doubt the affiliations of the victims, while the attackers were reported to have been linked with a hostel characterised by its support for Inkatha.

Typically, when the press analysed these events it sometimes had difficulty in coping with their political implications and content. For example, the *Guardian* featured two analyses of the Boipatong massacre. The first, by Rian Malan and Denis Beckett,[25] explained the event as revenge for an atrocity by the African National Congress, which sought out and killed Inkatha members in Boipatong on the night of Saturday 13 June—four days before the Boipatong massacre itself. They attributed the subsequent 'massacre of innocents' to an act of revenge by the residents of the nearby kwaMadala hostel where Zulu members of Inkatha lived.

The second, by David Beresford,[26] suggested instead that the event was vengeance triggered by the killing of a white police commander in the area, and he pointed to the evidence that the massacre was facilitated by the use of security force vehicles and that white gunmen were said by witnesses to be amongst the killers.

It is, however, the thesis of this analysis that these two explanations, whether taken separately or together—for they are not mutually inconsistent—are inadequate. For one thing, they both import an element of rationality which accounts of other similar incidents cannot offer: if the prior incidents are true, then while what occurred subsequently cannot possibly be justified, at least we would have an explanation as to why passions were aroused. This would make the Boipatong massacre unusual, for generally the press reports offered no such prior provocations to explain other massacres. Further, assuming that either or both of the two provocative incidents took place—and there is no reason to doubt that they did—the only link between them and the massacre, which we are asked to accept followed as a result, is that the victims lived in Boipatong. The attackers appear, from the press reports seen, to have made no effort to target those actually responsible—merely being a township resident justified being the victim of a revenge attack by Zulu-speaking, Inkatha-supporting hostel dwellers. Note that Malan and Beckett describe the victims as

---

Inquiry: Johannesburg.
25. *Guardian*, 30 June 1992.
26. *Guardian*, 3 July 1992.

'innocents'.

If these explanations based on provocation are correct then they put in doubt the entire process of change in South Africa for they seem to assume the existence of deeply-rooted grounds for conflict based on ethnicity and tensions between Zulus and others. They are thus consistent with and support the view of the former South African Government as expressed by 'Pik' Botha.[27] The inadequacy of ethnic-based explanations is emphasised when one bears in mind, as Taylor notes, that 'the conflict in Natal, ostensibly between Inkatha and the African National Congress, is not a Zulu-Xhosa clash; those killing each other are Zulus.'

Thus an analysis that depends on the reasons given by the former Minister, as quoted above, tends to support the preservation rather than the ending of apartheid. Taylor puts the matter bluntly:

> Interpreting (the violence) as a Zulu-Xhosa conflict articulates well with the ideology of South African multi-nationalism, absolves the state and those who benefit from it and dictates a law and order response...rather than one directed at addressing underlying material conditions.

It is argued here that accounts which do not locate the violence firmly in both the social structures created by apartheid as well as in the political processes of apartheid itself are at best incomplete and inadequate. We should ask whether other superficially inexplicable cases involving apparently random victims and the Boipatong massacre do not in fact have more similarities than differences, and whether the 'trigger' incidents in Boipatong merely formed the background, or even the camouflage, for what might or would have happened anyway. Certainly, there is much evidence that the residents of the kwaMadala Hostel in Boipatong were involved in violence before the massacre of 17 June 1992 and an attack by its inmates was anticipated.[28] A further, and not inconsistent, analysis is that the earlier killings in Boipatong merely supplied a pretext for what followed. In other words, they were a grotesque and disproportionate justification which, precisely because

---

27. Above, p. 29.
28. Vaal Council of Churches, *Memorandum by Lawyers Representing the Vaal Council of Churches: 'Efforts to Prevent the Boipatong Massacre'*; 23 June 1992.

it *was* grotesque and disproportionate, made Boipatong a suitable venue for yet another massacre, in the judgment of those whose interests were served thereby.

This suggests a degree of rationality and planning behind the Boipatong massacre and similar events. The alternative is to invoke an image of 'black on black' violence—mutually destructive conduct lacking even the thinnest of political motives, and occurring simply because it is part of the culture of black people to engage in it.

3 TOWARDS A THEORY FOR THE VIOLENCE

There is a danger, however, in seeking explanations which depend wholly on sociological conditions. Rupert Taylor, for example, offers a grim description of the living conditions for millions in the Vaal Triangle. There is no intention here to question the accuracy of his account, and indeed it gains in cogency by being based explicitly on the consequences of the entire apartheid policy. But by concentrating almost entirely on these social conditions he ignores the processes inherent in that policy: apartheid acquires a static rather than a dynamic quality, and the people become its passive victims even though they are the actors in the violence. It would be absurd to deny that the conditions and processes which Taylor describes are conducive to violence, but his conclusion does not allow sufficient space for the inherently violent nature of apartheid itself: violence is not merely the result of apartheid, but necessary for it. He writes:

> The conflict, in sum, is not of some essential ethnic (or 'tribal') forces, it is the fruit of apartheid. It reflects the extent to which the National Party, through apartheid, has succeeded in engineering group divisions amongst the oppressed.

The analysis is incomplete; saying that the deprivation and misery generated by apartheid, and which Taylor describes, have caused the victims to turn against each other does not take into account the evidence that apartheid has actually made use of violence to sustain itself. Taylor says:

Understanding the Nightmare: Politics and Violence in South Africa

> Years of apartheid policies have generated widespread deprivation and social fragmentation within the townships, causing endemic structural violence.

This is not a novel view, and there is overwhelming evidence to support hypotheses which link social deprivation and a high incidence of criminality. But in the South African context, as Taylor perceives it, this does not adequately refute the racist perspective of 'black on black' violence for it does not take into account the inherent violence of apartheid itself. He could be interpreted as saying that in all cases where the actors come from the very community which apartheid has ravaged, they are responding to their common misery by victimising each other—victims and perpetrators becoming indistinguishable from each other for the purpose of this analysis. The implication is that this is irrational self-destructive conduct, which is characteristic of the community in which it is located and thus needs no further explanation.

This, surely, is not the message which Taylor intends to give, for by coming so close to the 'black on black' perspective it weakens the impact of his final paragraph, where he points out (correctly, it is submitted) that this endangers the building of a new South Africa. It must be emphasised that absent from this critique of Taylor's thesis is any suggestion that he favours apartheid; on the contrary—the point being made is that his analysis, which is patently hostile to apartheid, does not penetrate deeply enough into the processes underlying the violence.

A different approach is taken by Morris and Hindson. They state:

> The harsh reality is that racial, ethnic and class antagonisms held in check under classic apartheid have resurfaced in the climate of liberalisation and deracialisation...Contrary to the expectations of many ordinary people and the predictions of a number of liberal social scientists, the gradual erosion of apartheid institutions and the abandonment of its policies has led to an escalation of social tensions and increased, not decreased, violence throughout the country. Along with the collapse of apartheid and the changing role of the state has come an ever increasing level of social chaos...

This is not, however, simply the 'black on black' thesis. They argue that it was not inevitable that moving from apartheid would produce the conflict and violence, but that it followed from the particular way the State chose to reform apartheid in the 1980s:

> 'Orderly urbanisation', without major state sponsored infrastructure programmes, exacerbated the material basis of conflict in black society. Relegating political rights for Africans to a minor say in local township affairs fundamentally politicised the conflict over the allocation of urban material resources.

Other factors inflaming the situation which they mention were conflicts and antagonisms over the allocation of social resources and threats to the Homeland elite from the prospect of the demise of the Homeland system. Listing the economic, social and political processes which accompany the disintegration of apartheid, they say:

> The roots of the violence must be sought not in the implementation of apartheid forms of social control but in the collapse of these forms; not in the continued maintenance of apartheid but in the attempted institutionalisation of a new social basis on the foundations of a racially divided society.

They continue with an exploration of tensions within black residential areas, and point to a model for the emergence of youth structures and warlords (which they claim were mostly allied to the African National Congress and to Inkatha, respectively) as part of the forces involved in local, regional, and national struggles for hegemony. The picture was complicated by the role of the police; Morris and Hindson note the evidence that these tended to support Inkatha, stressing that

> ...it is the break up of the cohesion of the state and the decomposition of central power and legitimacy that provides the context for these clandestine interventions by branches and individuals of the security forces at local and national level.

The writers also draw attention to the non-political violence:

> The breakdown of black social life, the absence of socially regulative mechanisms and the spiralling culture of violence

has spawned apolitical violent forces: gangs, crime syndicates, and mobsters. These are peopled with many who months previously were ranged on either side of the political divide. The gap between an Inkatha leader using an *impi* against African National Congress youth, and a warlord using an *impi* predominantly to settle scores, extort protection money and accumulate ill gotten wealth is extremely small...

They conclude that as time passes violence against the State and between competing political organisations degenerated into outright crime.

This may be a misleading simplification of the processes involved; they may be more complex than this view might suggest, and efforts to distinguish between what is 'politically-motivated' violence and what is not may be difficult if not pointless. It is interesting to compare their analysis with that of the ANC, which seems to have little doubt that the distinction between overtly political and so-called 'apolitical' violence is blurred. For example, the Secretarial Report to the 1992 Western Cape Regional Conference of the ANC, after reviewing the organisation's role in the solution of the taxi war during 1991 in the Capetown area, pointed to evidence that attempts were being made to revive this conflict and to link it to other violence. It drew attention to the 'new form of violence'—men wearing balaclavas who were 'robbing, mugging and killing our people in the middle of the night'. Evidence that this was political can be deduced from 'the lack of police investigation and interest in solving this problem' and that at the time of the report the only two people arrested were both former special constables. But what is more relevant to the observations by Morris and Hindson is that the report notes that there were allegations that in some areas African National Congress members were involved in criminal activities and that this had created very serious tensions and problems. The Report continues:[29]

> 37. Our position has been that if African National Congress members have been identified with these activities, they must be taken to the police, because these activities have

---

29. Secretarial Report to the 1992 Western Cape Regional Conference; see especially paragraph 30-38.

absolutely nothing to do with the struggle. In fact they are designed to give the organisation and the struggle a bad name. What is clear, is that we will not tolerate a situation where armed bands threaten, intimidate and even kill our members.

38. Gangster violence has this year alone taken about a dozen lives of our comrades or more, and both the coloured and African communities are groaning under the burden of these ruthless gangsters. Even those few who are arrested, are quickly released by the police. This may appear very strange, but it is understandable because the police seem to want to perpetuate tension and violence in our communities.

Independently, the *Weekly Mail* reported that according to 'township sources' there was a 'murderous armed gang of renegade ANC Youth League members' in Khayalitsha—at the heart of the area covered by the Secretarial Report quoted above. This gang, the *Weekly Mail* clearly implied, shot dead members of a committee elected by local residents from the ANC and from Khayalitsha's civic organisation which had been formed in order to ask the police for help, after attempts by the ANC to defuse the situation had failed.[30]

If these accounts about the Capetown region are typical—and there is no reason to doubt this—then it is not sufficient to describe political violence as 'degenerating into outright crime' for what appears to be 'apolitical' conduct is more likely to be powerfully driven by explicitly political motives. If this is so, then a simple repressive response by the state is not merely inadequate but likely to be grievously counter-productive.

Morris and Hindson offer a perspective on how the violence should be addressed. They reject what they describe as 'the neo-liberal path currently dominant'. This, they claim, accentuates class distinctions and this would perpetuate the 'primary antagonism' which characterises apartheid—the economic polarity between most whites and most blacks. The point must be made that central to their thesis is the role of workers and the trades unions. A great deal can be said about this perspective, but this essay is not the appropriate vehicle.

---

30. *Weekly Mail*, 18-22 December 1992. See also the *Weekly Mail*, 23-29 November 1992.

Understanding the Nightmare: Politics and Violence in South Africa

Morris and Hindson's analysis is altogether more complex and attempts to be more political than Taylor's, but in the final reckoning it is little more than a highly-dressed up version of the 'black on black' thesis. Indeed, they pose the question right at the very outset: why were blacks killing each other rather than whites at the time when apartheid was in its demise rather than at its peak? The underlying assumptions fatally flaw their analysis: apartheid was not in any decline at the time they wrote, and their argument that the distinctions it involved had altered and been replaced by others fails to explain what was happening. Further, despite offering a complex view of social forces operating within South African society, their discussion seems to be based on an assumption that the violence was something new, or at least that it had broken out because old controls had gone. To argue, as they do, that 'the roots of the violence should be sought in the effects of the disintegration of apartheid rather than its continued implementation' simply brushes aside the essential violence of apartheid. The violence was in fact nothing new; what was new was the public's concern with it. Further, because they do not focus on apartheid's need for violence, they cannot confront adequately the violence apartheid used: a violence which increased dramatically (rather than emerged for the first time—a crucial difference) in an effort to protect it when what seemed to be the final assault had begun. As a result, they cannot go further than state that it is not clear whether the activities of the security forces were part of the strategy of the De Klerk regime. On the other hand, had they based their discussion on the proposition that, still being a dynamic and active force, apartheid would actively seek to defend itself, a very different interpretation of the nature of the violence would have been offered. By claiming that 'endemic violence...was not a necessary consequence of the collapse of apartheid' the writers are, firstly, asserting that apartheid had collapsed—which it had not done—and secondly, giving credence to those who wish us to think that it had.

It is instructive to compare their words with those of 'Pik' Botha, quoted above.[31] The misconduct of the police and army, as they describe it, seems to be little more than an unfortunate aberration which, while serious when and to whom it occurred, was not central to the issue. The most cursory review of some of the characteristics of the

---

31. Above, p. 29.

violence used by these arms of the state reveals just how false this image actually is.

Finally, the emergence of politically-motivated and ostensibly random attacks on whites demonstrates that a 'black on black' model answers few, if any, questions. Whether or not the same organisation was responsible for the many killings and massacres in which the victims were black, as well as for incidents such as the grenade and machine gun attack on a largely white congregation in St James' Church in Kenilworth, Cape Town on 1 August 1993, it is clear that the same political objectives were being served—the preservation of the apartheid status quo.

The work of Simpson and Rauch[32] is altogether more persuasive than any of the other writers referred to, for they embed the entire phenomenon of the violence in a dynamic political structure far more successfully. They further lay the basis of an analysis which brings out the false dichotomy between political and non-political violence. They say:

> The unshackling of the political process...had the unintended consequence of 'deregulating the existing mechanisms of social control' without effectively replacing them with consensus-based alternatives. The highly repressive means of control which resulted in a substantially over-regulated society prior to 1990, were necessarily withdrawn to facilitate the envisaged process of negotiation. This served to erode existing perceptions of authority (whether legitimate or not) and rendered the institutions historically responsible for implementing these mechanisms of social control even less effective than had previously been the case...We refer to this process as the 'deregulation of social control' in the post-1990 period. Simply put, this amounts to the piecemeal deconstruction of social control under apartheid, without the immediate generation of viable alternatives. This process operates both institutionally and ideologically, serving to undermine historically dominant ideological and institutional authority within the society. It also operates materially, as competing claims to limited resources within the society become less constrained by the regulatory and repressive

---

32. Simpson and Rauch, above, note 1.

Understanding the Nightmare: Politics and Violence in South Africa

mechanisms which have historically entrenched limitations on people's expectations, social mobility and control over resources.

They talk of the breakdown, without any replacement by alternatives, of the apartheid structures responsible for administering the material elements of township life and the resultant significant decline in material standards of living. But their review does not stop at this point.

They also address, among other factors, the questions of violence flowing from the police and army, from a 'third force', and from the political right wing.

The state structures are discussed in the context of their histories; the writers show how the police, without credibility and almost completely untrusted, began at best to operate 'beyond the control of government; and, at worst, continued to pursue a long-established political agenda.'

In dealing with a 'third force' analysis—reflecting presumably the activities of structures operating outside of both the formal anti-apartheid groupings and of the State and its official agencies—they point to the need to distinguish between interests politically motivated to disrupt the peace process, and those concerned to maintain high levels of violent conflict. They talk of the emergence of a 'sub-economy' based on a trade in arms, assassinations, and protection rackets. They argue:

> Thus, whilst it is clear that there exist—within the ultra right-wing groupings, within the security establishment and even within some of the key political organisations—groupings with a political interest in disruption...these interest groups are reliant on the active engagement of materially-rooted interest groups as well.
>
> ...The arguments about politically motivated 'third force' involvement are the most easily sustained in relation to the assassination of political activists, particularly those strategically placed in relation to the unfolding peace process, or functional within its embryonic structures.

Simpson and Rauch reach a cautious conclusion, arguing that one must be clear as to how such a 'third force' is structured politically and

Negotiating Justice

what its objectives might be. They try to delineate its objectives:

> ...the generation of fear and increased conflict serves a direct interest, whilst being simultaneously functional to the processes of destabilisation of social control. The cumulative effect has clearly been a contribution to the unhinging of an already tentative negotiation process.

It is not possible, in the scope of this essay, to review the material and discuss the existence of a 'third force'; however, the question of collaboration and interaction between corrupt elements within the police, political organisations opposed to change, and 'ordinary' criminal elements is returned to below. Suffice it to say that the evidence is that there is unlikely to be a coherent and disciplined but concealed structure bent on wreaking havoc; it is more likely that various elements and factions with their own agendas, but embedded within visible organisations which are suffering from powerful internal tensions, form loose alliances according to repeated patterns. One may speculate that individual members of a demoralised police and army containing deeply corrupt elements, of a deeply-divided right wing lacking clear policies, objectives, and leadership, and of a powerful and established 'ordinary' criminal community, can frequently co-operate with each other on a 'project' basis; indeed, they may be the same people on occasion and their roles and the hats they wear may be confused. So far as the police are concerned, the image is of a force riddled with problems. The Waddington report on the police's handling of the Boipatong massacre, for example, can scarcely fill a conscientious officer with pride, and elsewhere in the work of the Goldstone Commission there are findings and comments which are hardly complimentary to say the least.[33] Another illustration is the Goniwe inquest in the Eastern Cape (probing the death of a group of ANC activists and other alleged 'hit squad' activity); here, senior

---

33. One of the most remarkable is in the 'Report on the Planning and Instigation of Acts of Violence by the Police in the Vaal Area'. The Commission found that allegations against the police in the *Weekly Mail* were unsupported by satisfactory evidence, and then said that: '...outside the evidence before this Committee there is much to suggest that in other contexts and in other circumstances covert operations have been abused in that they have been the means whereby illegal acts of violence have been carried out by the security forces'.

police officers can be seen pointing fingers at each other on the question of whether or not illegal activities including murder had been known of, ordered or carried out by the police. Various allegations do not have to be true for one to be tempted to conclude that there existed a web of mutual loathings and betrayals among those involved, and the tensions must surely have reverberated down to the lowest ranks. For example, on 23 June 1993 one witness, Colonel Winter, admitted that the police had access to the equipment used in Goniwe's murder and had known of his movements on the night of his death, but pointed out that the SADF also had the sophistication to carry out the murder.[34]

From these and a tidal wave of other indicators no less remarkable, one forms the impression of a police force in serious trouble.[35]

3.1 The Political Implications

There is evidence that an attempt was being made to use violence in lieu of law directly as a means of simple political control. The problem which this raises is to identify those responsible.

Until a late stage in its existence, the apartheid South African Government was able to rely on its massive security legislation, and in particular the Internal Security Act and Emergency Regulations, as its principal weapons against its political opponents. The African National Congress, the South African Communist Party, the Pan-African Congress, and other organisations were illegal, membership and support for their activities were serious crimes, and the frequent use of prolonged detention and other severe administrative measures against individuals made virtually every form of resistance to the Government dangerous indeed. However, in February 1990 it released the leadership, including Nelson Mandela, and many activists and members of illegal organisations. It thus became necessary immediately to remove the prohibitions on the organisations and the administrative

---

34. Probably the best running account of the protracted proceedings is the Monthly Repression Report published by the Human Rights Commission, which lists the Press reports on which the synopses are based.
35. Note especially the observations of the Report of the Commonwealth Observer Mission to South Africa, *Violence in South Africa*, Chapter 6; above, note 5.

weapons if there was to be any prospect of constitutional negotiations proceeding. In addition, the Government was forced to respond to pressure to end the state of emergency. The effect was to reduce in certain respects the availability of various types of detention, criminalisation, and other techniques of disabling the opposition.

Some of the political implications of this were noted by the Goldstone Commission of Inquiry Regarding the Prevention of Public Violence and Intimidation (hereafter, referred to as the Goldstone Commission). In the Second Interim Report, Judge Goldstone drew attention to the role of the police when considering the causes of violence. He noted that the State had legalised the 'large and predominantly black-supported political organisations' and continued:[36]

> This must be seen against a background of a lawful and largely Government-supported Inkatha Freedom Party having been at war with a largely underground African National Congress and its front organisations. With rapid change the Government, again suddenly and unexpectedly, resolved to negotiate in public and in private with organisations that were perceived, for good reason or bad, as the enemy of Inkatha, of White South Africans, and most important, of the police and army.

The Interim Report specifically listed,[37] as one of the causes of the violence

> A police force and army which, for many decades, have been the instruments of oppression by successive White Governments in maintaining a society predicated on racial discrimination.

Evidence to the effect that the South African Defence Force trained members of Inkatha as far back as 1986 was presented to the Goldstone Commission by the South African organisation Lawyers for Human Rights.[38] This was subsequently confirmed by the Goldstone

---

36. Goldstone Commission of Inquiry Regarding the Prevention of Public Violence and Intimidation, Second Interim Report, para. 2.3.3.
37. Goldstone Commission of Inquiry Regarding the Prevention of Public Violence and Intimidation, Second Interim Report, para. 2.3.2.
38. Lawyers for Human Rights, *Memorandum to the Goldstone Commission*, March 1992.

Understanding the Nightmare: Politics and Violence in South Africa

Commission, as has been mentioned above.[39] The organisation picked out the political objectives behind the formation and fostering of vigilantes and 'hit squads':

> Fundamental to the thinking underlying (this) strategy was the notion of contra-mobilisation involving the mobilisation of groups and sections of the population, their support and funding in order that such groups and persons should be in a position to attack targeted forces or organisations such as SWAPO in Namibia and the African National Congress and the United Democratic Front and their allies in the Republic thereby relieving the security forces of much of the burden of containing such organisations.

The Human Rights Commission observed that assassination created an atmosphere of terror, and forced leaders into hiding from where they could not longer operate effectively. Pointing out that in every opinion poll conducted after February 1990 the African National Congress had recorded an average of at least 70 per cent or more of black political support (as against, for example, an average of 1 per cent for Inkatha), in a joint paper prepared for the Human Rights Commission and Community Agency for Social Enquiry the two organisations remarked[40] that

> ...the violence makes it extremely difficult for the African National Congress to translate its support into an organised membership. Being unable to respond to calls for defence, the African National Congress is in danger of appearing weak and ineffectual in the eyes of township residents.

So far as can be determined, the authorities did not deny that 'hit-squads' existed. Following the disclosure that funds had been channelled through the South African Defence Force for training paramilitary 'hit-squad' units, the SADF issued a statement[41] that it was

> ...not prepared to comment in any way on allegations and

---

39. Above, p. 22.
40. Everatt, D. and Sadek, S. (1992) *The Reef Violence: Tribal War or Total Strategy?* joint paper for the Community Agency for Social Enquiry and the Human Rights Commission: Johannesburg.
41. *Weekly Mail* December 13-18, 1991.

speculations about covert actions which were authorised and carried out in the national interest.

This policy—of refusal to comment—extended to individuals. In similar vein, allegations of complicity in murder had been made against named, very senior, officers.[42]

It was not until December 1992 that President De Klerk acted, following a raid by agents of the Goldstone Commission on a secret headquarters of a military intelligence unit in which documents with details of the army's involvement in activities to discredit the ANC were discovered. At roughly the same time, further incriminating documents were revealed at an inquest into the assassination in 1989 of a prominent academic and anti-apartheid activist, David Webster. One detail which was disclosed is that President De Klerk himself assured the army that there would be no 'witch-hunt' into the activities of a murder squad it ran.[43] It is impossible to summarise here the information which was revealed by Judge Goldstone,[44] but the upshot was that President De Klerk announced that 23 senior officers were to be suspended or retired and announced further enquiries. He admitted that people had died as a result of these activities.[45] Judge Goldstone said that the operations involved associating the ANC with criminal activities, and that the police had hired a convicted murderer to handle the work as well as drug dealers, prostitutes, and homosexuals.

Evidence that the violence was carried out according to some overall

---

42. Perhaps the most extended and detailed is the biographical account and confession of Dirk Coetzee as researched and recounted by Pauw, J. *In the Heart of the Whore* (Southern Book Publishers, 1991, Halfway House). There have been allegations that during 1992 South African Police agents came to Britain, where Coetzee is in hiding, in a foiled attempt to kill him. They were picked up by British police and expelled. Coetzee has said, explicitly, that he was the commander of the South African Police death squad and claims that he and his men `had to' murder political and security opponents of the police and the Government.
43. *Guardian*, 23 November 1992.
44. See for example the following, which give various details, accounts, and analyses of developments: *Daily Telegraph*, 17 November 1992; *Guardian* 17 November 1992; *Times*, 17 November 1992; *Morning Star*, 18 November 1992; *Guardian*, 18 November 1992; *Guardian*, 20 November 1992; the *Weekly Mail* for 20-26 November, 1992 .
45. *Guardian*, 21 December 1992.

strategy is found when the timing of individual incidents is considered. The monthly frequency of incidents as collated by the Human Rights Commission appears to be random until one compares the numbers with the dates of important political developments in South Africa. There is, arguably, a dramatic rise when reports of bloodshed would cause the maximum harm to the opposition, and an equally dramatic drop when the image of the State, or of President De Klerk, or of other symbols or figures, would otherwise have been harmed.

The correlation is nothing less than startling. For example, in July 1990 the reported number of politically-related deaths was 144, countrywide. The historic 'Pretoria Minute' was signed the following month following a much-publicised meeting between the Government and the newly-unbanned anti-apartheid organisations and their released leadership including Nelson Mandela. The number of politically-related deaths rose that month to approximately 709. In September, during the start of the campaign by the African National Congress and other organisations for a constituent assembly, the figure fell to 369; but it was just 106 in October when F.W. De Klerk, then State President, visited Denmark and Ireland—which were at the forefront of the campaign in Europe for sanctions against South Africa.[46]

The South African experience of assassination confirms that its sheer ugliness renders it an inadequate and inefficient means of exercising political control. It generates martyrs, and its high visibility causes problems for its perpetrators in international relations and hardens domestic resistance. The process, in fact, is self-defeating and discredits all those responsible.

However, when combined with the misery of more general violence, assassination proved to be more effective in damaging the opposition in South Africa. What follows is an attempt to formulate a possible model which at least in part explains this process; until recently this was hypothetical for up to now there was no more than circumstantial evidence that any planning or conspiracy had been involved. One may

---

46. Graphical displays of the figures are provided in the joint paper prepared for the Community Agency for Social Enquiry and the Human Rights Commission by Everatt and Sadek, above, n. 40. The document remarks that the 'peaks and troughs' of the violence 'mirror the waxing and waning fortunes of the National Party Government, as it seeks to negotiate a future South Africa which retains minority control of economic and political power.'

feel that the state in particular had been derelict in confronting the issues, but this is a different matter from an assertion that there was a coherent policy of replacing the mere criminalisation of political opposition with the physical elimination of it.

3.2 A Model for the Violence

The combined effect of assassinations and massacres was, arguably, partially to disguise the political nature of assassinations and to make them seem instead to be unfortunate incidents in what could be represented as some sort of 'normal' environment of violence—exemplified in the speech of the former Minister of Foreign Affairs, 'Pik' Botha, when he told the Security Council that the violence was caused by ethnic tensions between the African National Congress and Inkatha.[47] At the same time, organised violence was used as a way of alienating the community from whom the victims of assassination were drawn. When the cost of associating with a targeted organisation can be measured in terms of becoming a victim of its political enemies, then hostility to that organisation can be engendered. The processes of camouflage, alienation, and provocation arising from the massacres combine with the obvious damage caused by assassinations, and the result is a picture of extensive violence which is sustained because it becomes self-perpetuating. In terms of this model, the camouflage process operates through the random choice of victims—and the more numerous, the better.

Simultaneously, the political context of what was happening could be emphasised by the perpetrators, making the penalty for political involvement high indeed. By attacking individuals at random within a community known to support a particular organisation, a form of collective punishment was imposed and people were terrorised into avoiding any support or contact with that which brought them such misery. It was not necessary for the victims to be members or supporters of the target organisation themselves; and paradoxically, as the South African experience seems to demonstrate, it was immaterial if the victims' conclusion that the attackers came from an organisation known to be hostile to the target organisation was erroneous; all that

---

47. Above, p. 29.

mattered was that they should have thought that this was the case. It was thus not illogical that police officers, members of political organisations, or criminal gangs might have posed as members of each other's structures or organisations if their objectives were to provoke violence and use terror and confusion. Reported connections between the killers and such organisations were frequently either absent or vague and uncertain, and if made were hotly disputed. It is striking that the police, the African National Congress and Inkatha all claimed to have been impersonated by the perpetrators of the violence. Certainly, so far as the police were concerned, the formidable 'Koevoet' ('Crowbar') unit, trained in precisely this sort of activity, had been transferred to, and was operational in, South Africa following the independence of Namibia where it had been established and where it engaged in 'pseudo-operations' against SWAPO.[48]

The processes of camouflage and intimidation described above are not necessarily in conflict with each other at all, and indeed can operate simultaneously even in the same incident. It all depends on what is suspected or known or disclosed to others—eyewitnesses, observers from the immediate community, and, through the press, the outside world. The report of killings in Soweto quoted earlier illustrates clearly this ambiguous quality and its impact. For example, survivors and others within the community may have known very clearly from their own information sources and experience what the true basis of the attack was—the terrorism motive was clear to them. But the press did not always report such incidents fully and the killings seemed to be just another apparently 'incomprehensible' incident in the overall pattern of violence.

It was clear that it was intended from the outset that those who felt themselves to be exposed to such attacks would retaliate or act pre-emptively. Where there were hostels, for example, from which the killers were thought to have come then these, and their inmates, became targets. A self-sustaining cycle of terror developed. The International Commission of Jurists drew attention to this process in its analysis of the massacre at Trust Feeds in 1988 (one of the very few massacres that came to trial). The judge had concluded that the police

---

48. For an outline of this and other recent policing issues and problems, see Cawthra, G., *South Africa's Police: From Police State to Democratic Policing?* (Catholic Institute for International Relations, 1992, London).

officer in command had intended that everyone in the house where the killings took place should be killed. The ICJ report continues:[49]

> Either by mistake—as the judge suggested—or by design—part of a strategy to stir up revenge killings, as the prosecution suggested—all 11 victims were Inkatha supporters.
>
> The incident was then covered up and the residents's association blamed for the attack. Members and supporters of the association could never set foot in Trust Feed again and Inkatha took over the township...

Allegations against the police and army reached such a pitch that it was inevitable that a proper investigation would eventually be mounted. Some of the claims were highly specific—the names of particular officers have been publicly linked with specific murders, for example—and there were repeated disclosures of funding and organisation by the police of so-called 'hit-squads' and other activities. Describing the allegations as amounting to a 'maelstrom', one account[50] describes funds being given to Gatsha Buthelezi to fund the training and deployment of a group which was used to assassinate African National Congress supporters. Mention has already been made of action taken by President De Klerk against a number of army officers. The Goldstone Commission heard evidence from an officer in the kwaZulu Police, describing the training and arms he was given by the South African Police in 1986 in order to kill non-Inkatha members.[51] It seems hardly necessary to claim that the worst possible conclusions which one might draw from what has become publicly known are justified.

In the context of the Boipatong massacre, it is impossible to ignore the explicit words of a report commissioned by the Goldstone Commission into the manner in which the police dealt with the incident. It was drawn up by Dr P.A.J. Waddington (the director of the Centre for Criminal Justice Studies at the University of Reading). It explicitly draws attention to the contrast between the treatment given by the police to the Boipatong victims and to the kwaMadala suspects.

---

49. International Commission of Jurists, *An Independent Survey of the Violence in South Africa* (1992).
50. *Guardian*, 6 February, 1992.

Understanding the Nightmare: Politics and Violence in South Africa

Dr Waddington describes the attempt by the police to justify themselves as 'difficult to accept', in view of their own account of the attitude of the residents to the police immediately after the event. He says, explicitly,[52] that the Boipatong residents

> might justifiably conclude that whereas their understandable anger and resentment was met with tear smoke, rubber bullets and bird shot, a similarly forceful attitude was not adopted towards the hostel-dwelling suspects. Whereas police were prepared to negotiate with hostel-dwellers, they avoided negotiating with representatives of the township.

The mass of circumstantial evidence has provoked Cawthra to claim:[53]

> Far from being removed from politics, the police have been central to the storm of political violence that has accompanied South Africa's transition to democracy... [S]ections of the police have acted as a 'third force', facilitating assassinations and massacres by anti-African National Congress forces that are designed to trigger cycles of violent retribution in black townships. They have aimed to weaken the African National Congress's organisational base, to raise the spectre of 'black-on-black' violence and to block progress towards a negotiated end to apartheid...

The Goldstone Commission and the United Nations together called for an investigation which would probe these matters. A partial enquiry, the Harms Commission, confirmed some fears but has been widely rejected as a whitewash owing to its very restricted terms of reference. By contrast, the Goldstone Commission had no such limitations imposed by the Peace Accord, which set it up. The Accord states that the Commission's objectives include inquiring 'into the phenomenon of public violence and intimidation in the Republic, the nature and causes thereof and what persons are involved therein'.

---

51. *Weekly Mail*, August 6-12, 1993; and see above, n. 22.
52. Waddington, Dr P.A.J, *Report of the inquiry into the police response to, and investigation of, events in Boipatong on 17 June 1992*: submitted to the Commission of Inquiry Regarding the Prevention of Public Violence and Intimidation (Goldstone).
53. Cawthra, G., p. 4; above, note 48.

3.3 Criminal Gangs

A worrying development was the involvement of what appeared to be criminal gangs which initially seemed to lack political objectives, but which were nevertheless recruited for these purposes on a mercenary basis. For example, there have been extensive reports and self-confessed criminal activity concerning a group known as the Black Cats,[54] including claims that the group was funded and protected by the police. A report by the Goldstone Commission into the involvement of the security forces in violence[55] confirmed that these accounts, and the group's close and active links with Inkatha, were all too true.

In the town of Kroonstad, the Three Million Gang was described by a member as having been helped by police, local councillors, and white businessmen with transport, weapons, and food. In this person's affidavit details are given of an assassination in which he participated in the presence of the police who were called to the scene by the leader of the gang using a two-way radio.[56]

Two leaders of a gang named 'Saddam 5' in a township near Bloemfontein claimed at a mass meeting that the gang was formed and registered at the local police station. The station commander said he had no comment to make about the gang's allegations. The meeting appears to have been called by angry residents because of the gang's alleged involvement in violence, murder, and hooliganism.

Once we accept that the apparently irrational and motiveless violence discussed earlier might, in fact, be politically driven then it is not fanciful to ask whether 'ordinary' crime and violence cannot be used for similar purposes. Certainly, if the allegations are correct, then corrupt police links with criminal gangs were established. The picture is deeply worrying.

---

54. *Guardian*, 24 January, 1992.
55. Published at the beginning of June 1993, but released by President De Klerk on 23 June; reviewed in the *Weekly Mail*, June 15-July 1 1993.
56. *New Nation*, 27 September-3 October, 1991.

4 WHITES AS VICTIMS

The violence described above is a picture in which the victims were, for the purposes of this discussion, black. In fact, all parts of the community experienced the violence and its related effects. If what is described above reflects efforts to prevent change, it is interesting to note that it is possible also to use the white experience for the same purpose. Indeed, it is in the interests of any who oppose constitutional change that *all* parts of the community should feel threatened.

It is not difficult to find, in the white-directed press, illustrations of how one can play on white fears. For example, the main story on the front page of a randomly selected edition of the Afrikaans-language daily published in the Transvaal,[57] strongly pro-apartheid, carried an article which reads (translated from the Afrikaans):

> Farmers in the (Orange) Free State are planning the 'biggest emergency meeting yet' in the province to put an end to the plundering, robbery, and theft on farms and in the rural areas.
>
> The police and army are also going to be drawn into the discussions, which will take place in Bloemfontein...
>
> Dr. Pieter Gouws, the new president of the Free State Agricultural Union, says that a 'low-level war' is being waged against farmers, particularly those near squatter-camps, black towns, and Lesotho.
>
> Many Free State (residents) now live in fear after numerous cases of murder, robbery and assault. They say they are being threatened and everything they possess is being stolen (*Note:* the original uses the lurid idiom '*rot en kaal gesteel*').
>
> The market value of farms has also declined sharply. In some districts farmers who have left their land cannot rent their farms...
>
> "There will have to be immediate talks with Lesotho", said Dr. Gouws. "The progressive conquest ('*verowering*') of white farms through theft is a fact."

---

57. *Transvaler*, 13 December 1991; the edition was published on the date that I had chosen, just under a year earlier, to fly from Johannesburg to London by South African Airways, and was read because it was available on the jet.

Negotiating Justice

> Clocolan's District Farmers' Union has already this week consulted the disaster and emergency aid committee of the Free State Agricultural Union about the stealing, robbery, and attacks.
>
> A memorandum has also been sent to the security forces.

Clearly, the message is that white safety can be assured only by apartheid.

Quite separate was the continued commitment of some political groups to the continuation of the armed struggle against the State. The decision by the military wing of the Pan-Africanist Congress to end this commitment during June 1993 made a material contribution towards reducing this cause of tension. One effect was to isolate those who supported a violent resolution to South Africa's problems.

5 CONCLUSIONS

One obvious question which must be considered is whether we are not looking at a pattern of senseless violence but dealing instead with deliberate policy prepared and executed by those with power and resources. The answer is not easy. It is tempting to point to a state conspiracy for which the evidence seems to be abundant and mounting, but there is some doubt that the previous Government was content to follow a policy of violence which it may have inherited from its predecessor. There has, for example, been a claim that the predecessor to ex-President De Klerk, P.W. Botha, admitted that he had sanctioned the assassination of more than 1000 black activists,[58] and De Klerk duly ordered an investigation—which appears to have been forgotten about—into this; but it is difficult to see how the South African Government today could sustain its involvement in such policies if it hoped to participate in processes of change which it had been forced into by the sheer weight of the opposition, national and international, with which it had to contend. On the other hand, it is even harder to see how the Government could sustain its denial of responsibility if it

---

58. Statement made by Mr Jan van Eck, Member of the House of Assembly; *Independent*, 28 May 1992.

Understanding the Nightmare: Politics and Violence in South Africa

failed to respond to that evidence. It is worth noting the careful words of Judge Goldstone in a statement made at the preliminary hearing into the Boipatong massacre:

> No evidence has been submitted to the Commission which in any way justifies allegations of any direct complicity in or planning of current violence by the State President, any member of the Cabinet or any highly placed officer in the South African Police or Defence Force. But if such evidence is submitted to the Commission it will be thoroughly investigated.

This must have created profound problems for the police in the light of the evidence already available. It must have been extraordinarily difficult for the South African Police to maintain morale and discipline when there were conflicts created by such uncertainties. Cawthra,[59] tracing the evolution of policing ideology in recent years in South Africa, draws attention to the total and instantaneous reversal of the role and self-perception of the police force from the beginning of 1990, when the release of Nelson Mandela and the other leaders, and the removal of the bans on the African National Congress and other organisations, took place. It became necessary for President De Klerk to tell them that whereas previously they had acted as 'a control function connected to a specific political party', their duties were now quite different:

> You will no longer be required to prevent people from gathering to canvass support for their views. This is the political arena and we want to take the police out of it. We don't want to use you any more to reach certain political goals...

This must have been a bewildering, even a shocking, development to many serving police officers. The failure to deny claims that very senior, named, officers ordered the murder of political figures, and the volume and detail of claims that the police continued to play a key role in the fomentation of violence, raise the question of whether De Klerk's instructions were repudiated rather than heeded. The social and

---

59. Cawthra, G., p. 3; above, note 48.

political conditions existed under which fearful corruption and criminality in the police might flourish. There is no reason to think that the South African Police were immune from processes that have characterised other societies in a state of transition. Disclosures of police misconduct must be seen in this light.

It would have taken little effort to make the vicious circle spin faster: to make 'ordinary' assault and killing, robbery, rape, burglary and theft—whether for gain or self-gratification—seem to be more 'normal' than ever. Cawthra[60] has drawn attention to the process whereby policing of what he calls 'normal' crime was displaced during the states of emergency between 1985 and 1990 by a preoccupation with 'ideological criminals'. He continues,

> As a result, crime prevention, especially in black areas, has been neglected and it has risen dramatically in the 1990's. For example, murders in 1990 increased by over 30 per cent to 15,109, only some of which could be attributed to the political violence.

The violence was truly frightening.

There are many implications arising from the above examination. Not the least was for urgent steps to be taken to secure proper policing. This paper is not the proper context for a discussion on whether the existing police could be reformed or be replaced by something wholly new. Either way, it hardly seems to be unreasonable to say that on this point alone action was urgent.

The Peace Accord,[61] drawn up in September 1991 and signed by the Government, the National Party, the African National Congress and many other organisations, set up a complex and far-reaching set of structures to address the violence. Its importance and potential cannot be overstated, and it deserves and must be given extended study and analysis. One of its most remarkable features was that it was a treaty between political and other organisations, the then ruling party, and the State in which the latter bound itself to take important steps—not the least of which was an undertaking to comply with the law. The question of the extent to which the Accord was legally enforceable seems to have been sidestepped by the appointment, in his official

---

60. Cawthra, G., p. 6; above, note 48.
61. For a fuller consideration of its work see Midgley, this book, Chapter 5.

capacity, of a senior judge to carry out functions defined by it. Certainly, Judge Goldstone made it clear that he expected the State in particular to give effect to conclusions the Commission reached which were within its remit and jurisdiction. For example, he reacted strongly to a failure by the State to give effect to recommendations he made on certain steps to be taken in regard to the hostels.

The Goldstone Commission was thus but one of the manifestations of the Peace Accord. It was a hopeful development that the United Nations was drawn in to assist in its implementation.

For the South African Police, the Accord is a most important matter. Properly applied by them, it must affect drastically not merely what they do but their accountability within the country as a whole.

The overall picture is thus, potentially, one that gives reason for hope for increasingly peaceful management of South Africa's problems. Never before in South Africa has a policy been established which united both the Government and the anti-apartheid opposition. The history and novelty of the Peace Accord break the mould of previous efforts to resolve South Africa's problems; this was the first time that the then Government committed itself to a legislative and administrative programme which the opposition totally supported. Indeed, in some respects the Peace Accord and the anxiety on the part of its signatories to reach a consensus might have served well as a model for the constitution-making process, and some of its terms would not be inappropriate in a democratic constitution itself.

Chapter Three

Constitution-Making: In Search of a Democratic South Africa

Nico Steytler

1 INTRODUCTION

It is trite to say that South Africa is in the process of transition. What is not easy to say is where the transition is leading. If the goal is a democratic state, then the *grundnorm or basic law* on which the State is to be built, must be democratic in process and content. This means that a supreme law, the constitution, should be written by the people. This can best be done by a constitution-writing body which is representative of the people by being freely and fairly elected. It is important, however, that this body should have the power to write the constitution.

These basic principles for the foundation of a democratic State sound trite, but in the South African context each one was fiercely contested. Although an election for a constituent assembly was agreed upon by 'sufficient consensus' at the Multi-Party Negotiating Council, held on 27 April 1994, the validity of this decision was challenged in court.[1] Throughout most of 1993 the powers of the constitution-making body were the subject of negotiations, and no final agreement was reached about what South Africa was and, consequently, who would vote in the election. Furthermore, the process to ensure a free and fair election was also highly contested.

---

1. A challenge in the Transvaal Provincial Division of the Supreme Court has been lodged by the Inkatha Freedom Party, *Cape Argus* 29 July 1993.

Constitution-Making: In Search of a Democratic South Africa

The disputes were informed not only by different conceptions of democracy but also by the immediate political interests of the main political players. This paper will argue that the manner in which these issues will be resolved will be indicative of whether a fully-fledged democratic state will emerge in South Africa. Compromises will inevitably be made[2] but if the essence of democracy is fundamentally compromised then a legitimate democratic state will not easily materialize.

2 AN ELECTED CONSTITUTION-MAKING BODY

The African National Congress has demanded from the outset a constituent assembly which would be charged with the task of drafting a new constitution. In the Harare Declaration of August 1989, the ANC set out the demand clearly. At the Convention for a Democratic South Africa (CODESA) the ANC proposed that the drafting and adoption of a new constitution could only be done by an elected body.[3] The argument is simply that a democratic state can only be built on a firm democratic basis. The people of South Africa, through their elected representatives at a constituent assembly, must write their own constitution.[4]

After the unbanning of the ANC on 2 February 1990 the South African Government resisted this idea vigorously, proposing instead a

---

2. Compromises on majority rule in order to establish democracy is not a new phenomenon. The politics of transition from autocratic to democratic rule through political pacts are evidence of this. For the sake of stability which a pact produces, greater democratization is abandoned. See generally Anderson, L., 'Political Pacts, Liberalism and Democracy: The Tunisian National Act of 1988' *Government and Opposition* 26, (1991) 244; Hagopian, F., '"Democracy by Undemocratic Means"? Elites, Political Pacts and Regime Transition in Brazil' *Comparative Political Studies* 23, (1990) 147; Karl, T. L., 'Petroleum and Political Pacts: The Transition to Democracy in Venezuela' in O'Donnell, G., Schmitter, P., and Whitehead, L., (eds) *Transitions from Authoritarian Rule in Latin America* (Johns Hopkins University Press, Baltimore, Md, 1986) p. 38.
3. Cachalia, F., 'Report on the Convention for a Democratic South Africa' *South African Journal on Human Rights* 9, (1992) 249, 257.
4. *Cf.* Sachs, A.L., *Protecting Human Rights in a New South Africa* (Oxford University Press, Cape Town, 1991) p. 1.

multi-party negotiating forum where all political parties, without regard to their possible electoral support, would agree by consensus on a new constitution. Such a constitution could then be subjected to popular approval by means of a referendum. The advantage for the Government was obvious. It, with its allies (the Homeland regimes and other parties in the tricameral parliament), could have made constitutional deals disproportionate to their possible electoral support. In January 1992 Dr Viljoen, the then chief Government negotiator at CODESA, said that[5]

> [I]f the interim constitution negtiated at CODESA was of such a nature that all the parties agreed that it was a 'good one' for a new South Africa, it could become the final constitution with the transitional Government leaders agreeing to extend its life and adopt it as a permanent constitution.

In May 1992 the Government rejected the ANC proposals to CODESA as being 'basically majoritarian' and stated that it would accept an elected constitution-making body if it is[6]

> constituted in terms of an interim transitional constitution agreed to in CODESA I and if it is bicameral in form, consisting of one chamber based on proportional representation and a second chamber based on regional and minority political party representation.

After CODESA II reached deadlock in May 1992, the Government accepted the principle of a constituent assembly in September in terms of the bilateral agreement between it and the ANC called the Record of Understanding.[7] Again the notion of a fully democratic constitution-making body was accepted with reservations. The constituent assembly, President De Klerk demanded, had to be bound by agreement in advance with a number of principles which included strong and entrenched regional government and power-sharing at the executive

---

5. *Business Day*, 29 January 1992; quoted in Cachalia, above, n. 3., 258.
6. Quoted in Cachalia, *op. cit.*, 258.
7. First mooted in bilateral talks between Cyril Ramaphosa, secretary general of, and chief negotiator for, the ANC; and Roelf Meyer, chief negotiator for the National Party (NP), *Weekly Mail* 4-10 October 1992.

Constitution-Making: In Search of a Democratic South Africa

level.[8] Agreement on a constituent assembly had now been reached to the extent that the Multi-Party Negotiating Council could agree by 'sufficient consensus' on the election date of 27 April 1994.

The Inkatha Freedom Party (IFP) at CODESA was consistent in its rejection of an elected constituent assembly.[9] This was coupled with a strong insistence on a federal form of government. In the 'Constitution of the State of KwaZulu/Natal' adopted by the kwaZulu Legislative Assembly on 1 December 1992, consociationalism was paraded under the mantle of federalism, with strong secessionist undertones.[10] At the Multi-Party Negotiating Council, the Concerned South African Group (COSAG) (which included the Inkatha Freedom Party, the Conservative Party (CP), and the governments of the Ciskei and Bophutatswana) rejected the idea of a constituent assembly[11] and consequently the election date of 27 April 1994.[12] They also filed an application in the Transvaal Supreme Court to have the election date set aside.[13]

The dispute about whether there should be an election was a dispute about democracy: whether the majority of the people expresses the will of the people of South Africa. As one political commentator observed, the deadlock between the NP and the ANC at CODESA II was about the failure of the NP to cross the democratic threshold.[14] Underlying the resistance to a democracy was the rejection of the unity of the South African nation. The ANC's declared position was that South Africa is one nation. In the Freedom Charter this idea was expressed in the preamble as follows: 'South Africa belongs to all who live in it, black and white'.[15] On the other hand, the National Party Government and its allies saw South Africa as comprising minorities, not a unified nation. This occurred within the context of race (in the case of the NP

---

8. *Weekly Mail* 16-22 October 1992.
9. Cachalia, above, n. 3, 258.
10. Ellmann, S. 'Federalism Awry: The Structure of Government in the kwaZulu/Natal Constitution', *South African Journal on Human Rights* 9 (1993) p. 165.
11. *Weekly Mail* 12-18 March 1993.
12. *Cape Argus* 4 June 1993.
13. *Cape Argus* 29 July 1993.
14. Philip van Niekerk, *Weekly Mail* 16-22 October 1992.
15. See further Steytler, N.C., 'Introduction' in N.C. Steytler (ed.) *The Freedom Charter and Beyond* (Wyvern, Cape Town, 1991) p. xi.

and CP) or ethnicity (in the case of Inkatha). It was therefore not surprising that the CP and Inkatha coalesced in a unified lobby to attempt to scupper the election. At stake was the unified view of the South African nation.

Political theorists argue that the purpose of elections is to ensure either the orderly transfer of power from one group to another or, in the event of the incumbent powerholder returning to office, the legitimation of its continued rule.[16] It is thus said that 'Elections are about public choices over who should rule, why, and under which political arrangements or government structures'.[17] The essence of democratic elections is that they must be real in their consequences; the elected representatives must have power.

The agreement between the Government and the ANC that there would be an election for a constituent assembly had been the result of a long and hard struggle since the unbanning of the ANC. When the Government relented on the demand for a constituent assembly, it did not entail embracing the ANC's concept of democracy. It saw the constituent assembly not as an authentic legislative forum in which the voice of the people could give expression to a new *grundnorm,* but as some sort of ratification device for a constitution drawn up elsewhere.

The central question was seen to be whether the constituent assembly would be able to write a constitution as it pleased. First the question would be whether there would be a minority veto of say 33.3 per cent. This is not an unusual procedure, as in many countries constitution-making has required greater consensus than a simple majority. Namibia is such an example where a two thirds majority was required for the drafting of the constitution.[18]

The second, and more important question, was whether the constituent assembly would have a free hand even with a 66.6 per cent

---

16. Maipose, G. S., 'The Electoral System of Zambia: The Conduct, Issues and Lessons', unpublished paper, Conference on Election Law, University of Botswana, March 1993.
17. Moyo, J. N., *Voting for Democracy: Electoral Politics in Zimbabwe* (Harare: University of Zimbabwe Press, 1992) 43.
18. See Erasmus, G., 'Die Grondwet van Namibië: Internasionale Proses en Inhoud' *Stellenbosch Law Review* 1 (1990) p. 277; Wiechers, M., 'Namibia: The 1982 Constitutional Principles and their Legal Significance', in D. van Wyk, M. and & Hill, R. (eds) *Namibia: Constitutional and International Issues* (Verloren van Themaat Centre for International Law, Pretoria, 1991).

majority to adopt any constitutional dispensation. The Government's aim was to write as much of the constitution as possible before the election, while they wielded an inordinate amount of power as the government in office. The ANC's position, on the other hand, was to agree to as little as possible before the election, and to wait for the constituent assembly as the proper forum to negotiate a constitution, because it would be there that their strength would lie as the most popular party in the country.

The most controversial constraints within which a constituent assembly would have to operate are the nature of the state, whether federal/regional or central, and the form of the executive Government.

The ANC broke the deadlock in the negotiations with the proposal of a government of national unity after the election. Joe Slovo, chairperson of the South African Communist Party (SACP), first suggested the inclusion in the new constitution of 'sunset clauses', whereby, all major parties would be included in the executive for a limited period immediately following the adoption of the constitution.[19] After heated debate within the ANC, the National Working Committee adopted the position.[20] The NP instead proposed the entrenchment of executive power-sharing on a permanent basis.[21] It proposed an elaborate scheme in the form of a Council of State to advise the State President who would be the leader of the most popular party. Parties with 10 per cent of the vote would get one seat on the Council of State while every party with 5 per cent of the vote get one cabinet post.[22] The underlying idea was that the proposed Council of State would be an inner cabinet or executive committee in which all the major role players would be represented. They would decide on policy principles on which cooperation within Government would be based. Moreover, decisions would be taken by consensus.[23] The Government's position remained in flux and the demand for permanent power-sharing, which was viewed as a serious obstacle, was quietly dropped in June 1993; the NP did not insist that permanent power-sharing be entrenched as a

---

19. *Weekly Mail* 30 October-5 November 1992.
20. *Weekly Mail* 20-26 November 1992.
21. *Weekly Mail* 16-22 October 1992.
22. *Weekly Mail* 21-27 May 1993.
23. *Financial Times* (London) 26 May 1993 as quoted in *Weekly Mail* 11-17 June 1993.

constitutional principle which would bind the constituent assembly.[24]

At the same time the ANC accepted that constitutional principles would be adopted by the Multi-Party Negotiating Forum which would set the parameters of the new constitution. It would inevitably mean that the room within which the ANC could manoeuvre would be limited. The effect of this concession was that the 26 political parties at the Forum, and not the democratically elected constituent assembly, would be taking important decisions, about such matters as the structure of the state.[25] Jan Gagiano, a political scientist, commented that one was witnessing the incremental writing of the constitution. The constituent assembly would now be left with filling in the details of the new constitution while the parameters of its powers had been circumscribed by the Forum.[26]

The regional/federal nature of a future constitutional dispensation appeared, in July 1993, to have been accepted by most major role players. One of the constitutional principles read that 'Government shall be structured at national, SPR and local levels'.[27] 'SPR', Chris Louw wryly commented, was 'CODESA-speak for 'states/provinces/regions'—a concept that had to be introduced so as not to antagonise confederalists, separatists, federalists or unitarists among the negotiators'.[28] The principle of SPR was an acceptance of a strong regional government as a minimum. Whether it would be more in accordance with a federal model, as Inkatha demanded, would be one of the issues to be resolved.

The elections should thus be seen in the following context: firstly, the elected constituent assembly would have limited powers, and secondly, an election would be fought between parties who then, after the fight, would have to kiss and make up in order to form an effective government of national unity. This is not to suggest that the election would be meaningless. On the contrary, it would be immensely important for parties to establish their legitimacy as the representatives of the people and thereby increase their clout in the constituent

---

24. *Weekly Mail* 18-24 June 1993.
25. *Weekly Mail* 21-27 May 1993.
26. *Ibid.*
27. Constitution of the Republic of South Africa 1993 (Draft outline: 21 July 1993); Schedule 1, XV. Eight Report of the Technical Committee on Constitutional Issues to the Negotiating Council, 26 July 1993.
28. *Weekly Mail & Guardian* 20 July-5 August 1993.

assembly and government of national unity.

Underlying the conflict about the power of the constituent assembly lay two competing views of representative democracy: an authentic and original lawmaker or a ratificatory and legitimating device for decisions made elsewhere. A party's preference for a particular concept of democracy coincided also with its expected electoral support in such a constitution-making assembly.

2.1 Who are the *Demos*?

At the core of democracy is the *demos*, the people. Democracy is often reduced to the ringing phrase: government by the people for the people. It assumes, however, that there is consensus about who the people are. In the period after 1990 there was no agreement on what South Africa was and consequently who *the people*, the voters, of South Africa were.

The struggle against apartheid was waged against all its manifestations, including the so-called 'independent' Homelands of Transkei, Bophutatswana, Venda and Ciskei (the 'TBVC' Homelands). The struggle was premised on the unitary nature of South Africa and that all the inhabitants of this territory were South Africans. The ANC thus demanded that all citizens of the 'independent' Homelands should vote in the first and most crucial election.[29] This would mean, *inter alia*, that an additional 5 million blacks would participate in the election. More particularly, the most populated Homeland, the Transkei, would vote solidly for the ANC.

The white Government's view was predictable. The aim of the grand apartheid scheme was the disenfranchisement of all Africans by stripping them of their South African citizenship. The cynical goal was to win, in the end, the numbers game; in South Africa whites would become numerically the majority. The Government argued that the issue of the Homelands should be dealt with by the new government *after* the election and the adoption of a new constitution. The new government should then negotiate with the Homelands about their reincorporation into South Africa. Two of the four Homeland regimes

---

29. Nogxina, S., and Pikoli V., 'A Comparative Survey and Lessons for South Africa' in *Electoral Laws in Transitional Arrangements* 10 (1993).

(Bophutatswana and Ciskei) were in complete agreement; so much so that these governments eventually abandoned the Government's fold and formed an alliance with the Conservative Party in the form of the COSAG alliance.

The first issue that had to be determined was whether citizens of the 'independent' Homelands could vote. If they could not, then grand apartheid would have been victorious at the very moment of its demise. The Government had moved away from a position that all citizens of the Homelands were not South African citizens. They could apply for their South African citizenship. Thousands had done after they had lived in South Africa for a period of 5 years, but the majority had not. The question that remained to be solved was whether citizens of the TBVC Homelands would automatically be regarded as South African citizens for the purposes of the elections?

Early in 1993 it seemed unlikely that the TBVC Homelands would be incorporated into South Africa before the April election. Even if their citizens were regarded as South African citizens, the question remained whether they would be able to vote in the Homelands. Would the Independent Election Commission, administering the elections, also assume control of the election process in the Homelands? Who would control the state-owned media and the security forces in the Homelands?

At CODESA II the issue of the Homelands was dealt with in the following way:

> Their participation will be arranged in such a way that their votes in a national election shall signify support for or rejection of re-incorporation. The result of such an election shall constitute a sufficient test of the will of the people.[30]

If this solution were to be adopted then their votes would not count towards the composition of the constituent assembly, but merely prove the obvious—whether or not they had rejected the illegitimate Homeland regimes. The ANC did not accept this position,[31] and in their proposed Transition to Democracy Act the Homelands were

---

30. Report of CODESA Working Group 4, para 3.1.3.
31. Maduna, P., 'Towards Democratic Elections in South Africa' in *Electoral Law in Transitional Arrangements* (Centre for Development Studies, Bellville, 1993), 24.

incorporated before an election.[32]

The position remained fluid, with progress towards incorporation often dictated by partisan interests. In February 1993 the South African Government agreed that the Homelands be incorporated and that their inhabitants be allowed to vote as South Africans.[33] In April the Government threatened to revoke unilaterally the independence of the Transkei, Ciskei and Venda in order to resume control over the territories and thereby combat the terror activities of the Pan Africanist Congress' military wing, APLA. At a time when the Government was moving towards the incorporation of the Homelands, resistance was coming from unexpected quarters. The Transkei Government, contrary to previous positions, came out against incorporation before election. Bantu Holomisa, the leader of the military government, said that he did not wish to be incorporated into apartheid South Africa, and the ANC seemed to be accepting this position.[34]

What was emerging in the negotiations were the contested contours of South Africa. The 'independent' Homelands appeared to have a life continuing past the collapse of grand apartheid. In the case of Bophutatswana there was a tenacious insistence on the continuance of independence. Transkei also resisted immediate incorporation for diametrically different political reasons. KwaZulu, which had hitherto refused the 'independence' offered by Pretoria, now threatened independence through secession. The notion of a South African people, collectively exercising the right to vote in pursuit of a common destiny, was proving difficult to establish in the machinations of *real politik*.

2.2 Ensuring Democratic Elections

For a constitution-making body to have any credibility (always assuming that the limited powers of the body and the fact that not everyone was represented there did not undermine its status) the election of its membership should be free and fair. A number of state institutions are usually involved in the election either directly or indirectly, namely, the Department of Home Affairs, the courts, the

---

32. *Weekly Mail* 4-10 September 1993.
33. *Weekly Mail* 12-18 February 1993.
34. *Weekly Mail* 23-29 July 1993.

state-owned media and the security forces. In the South African context the role of these institutions in the forthcoming election was highly contentious. At the heart of this issue lay the contestation over legitimate authority in South Africa.

2.2.1 Election Administration

The Government's position was clear: it was the legal authority in South Africa and the task of conducting the election fell to the state apparatus. Moreover, with years of experience in administering limited democracy in white politics it had the skills to administer an election competently. Already, in a cabinet reshuffle in February 1993, the new minister of Home Affairs, Danie Schutte, was hailed as the person who would be responsible for the holding of free and fair elections. Even after the principle of an Independent Election Commission (IEC) was conceded,[35] the Department of Home Affairs announced that the Government would be launching a voter education programme.[36] The Independent Forum for Electoral Education (IFEE) objected strongly against this programme, arguing that the Government should have no direct role in the election.[37]

The ANC's position was the opposite. The Government might be the legal authority in the country, but the struggle against the Government was precisely because it lacked any legitimacy to act as a credible and competent authority for all South Africans. The question of legitimacy did not simply refer to the illegitimate foundation of the South African state, but more practically to the Government's lack of credibility to administer the elections honestly. Simply put, the Government, which would be one of the main contestants in the election, could not be player and umpire at the same time. Moreover, the elections would have to be conducted in such a way that there could be no questioning of their legitimacy which in turn may influence the acceptance of the results.[38]

The ANC therefore suggested that an Independent Election

---

35. See below, p. 73.
36. *Weekly Mail* 11-17 June 1993.
37. *Ibid.*
38. *Weekend Argus* 9/10 January 1993.

Constitution-Making: In Search of a Democratic South Africa

Commission be appointed which would supervise and certificate the election.[39] Furthermore, the international community should be full members of such a commission. What was clear was that the Department of Home Affairs should be divested of all powers relevant to the conduct of the elections.[40] The commission should comprise a small number of eminent South Africans drawn from all the political parties.[41]

The Government's first response was that it would accept an independent election commission but it would be of limited significance. Its role would be to advise the Department of Home Affairs, much like the Advisory Election Commission in Zimbabwe.[42] Furthermore, the international community would play no role in the commission.

Agreement was eventually reached that there would be an Independent Election Commission (IEC). At the Multi-Party Negotiating Forum an IEC was proposed which would have the final say on all electoral matters.[43] The IEC would be responsible for the administration of the election as well as the adjudication of any disputes that might arise during or after the election.

Credible elections and competent election administrators are synonymous.[44] The key to any confidence the public might have in the outcome of an election also would lie in their confidence in the competency and impartiality of the election administration machinery.[45] A workforce of 90,000 persons would be required to be presiding officers, returning officers, counting officers, etc. Where would the IEC draw the election administrators from if officials from the Department of Home Affairs were not acceptable? The usual practice in apartheid elections had been to draw personnel from the civil

---

39. ANC, *Ready to Govern: ANC Policy Guidelines for a Democratic South Africa* (Centre for Development Studies, Bellville, 1992) 12.
40. Maduna, P., above, n. 31, p. 21.
41. Nogxina and Pikoli, above, n. 29, p. 12.
42. Moyo, J. N., above, n. 17.
43. *Cape Argus* 25 May 1993.
44. Mackenzie, W. J. M., and Robinson, K., (eds) *Five Elections in Africa: A Group of Election Studies* (Clarendon Press, Oxford, 1960)
45. Ntsabane, T., 'Issues and Debates in Botswana Electoral System' unpublished paper, Conference on Free and Fair Elections, University of Botswana, March 1993.

service, particularly magistrates as presiding and returning officers. In other African countries the presiding officer was usually the local headmaster of the senior secondary school, while teachers performed the duties of counting officers.[46]

All these categories of persons were contested. With a discredited magistracy, returning officers would have to be sought from other quarters. Filling this gap with school teachers might also prove problematic. When at a recent conference on free and fair elections,[47] it was suggested that headmasters of black high schools be used as elections officers, many black members of the audience howled with laughter. When questioned later by a puzzled political scientist who made the suggestion, they said that in the black communities the headmasters and teachers are perceived to be the most corrupt of all civil servants. What was therefore required were persons who would have the confidence of the whole community. With the civil services excluded, it was necessary to turn to civil society to find impartial persons of integrity and respect.

The method of resolving any election dispute was also contested. The African National Congress argued that the appropriate body should be the IEC which should make the final decision on any matter relating to the election.[48] The effect of the proposal was to exclude the South African Supreme Court from the process. The proposal flowed from concerns of practice and principle. Firstly, disputes during the election period over election issues need to be resolved expeditiously. The Supreme Court was not equipped or designed to resolve disputes quickly and expeditiously. Secondly, the very composition and ethos of the courts, made them part of the illegitimate state machinery. The Government, of course, would hold the opposite view.

The IEC proposal to the Multi-Party Negotiating Council included the provision that the IEC would have an electoral adjudicatory directorate which would be the final arbiter in disputes about the conduct of the election campaign or the election result.[49] The

---

46. Moyo, J. N., above, n. 17.
47. Conference on Free and Fair Elections, organised by the Centre for Development Studies and National Democratic Institute of International Affairs, Bellville, 12-14 March 1993.
48. Nongxina & Pikoli, above, n. 29, p. 16.
49. *Cape Argus* 25 May 1993.

Negotiating Council further accepted the recommendation of the Technical Committee on the IEC that a change in the composition of the IEC should be done in the same way as an amendment to the proposed constitution.[50] Again the existing judiciary proved to be contentious. The Technical Committee of the Multi-Party Negotiating Council recommended that judges adjudicate on matters such as appointment and termination of membership to the IEC. Penuel Maduna, an ANC negotiator, objected to this proposal stating that South African judges were all white and predominantly male which placed a question mark over their objectivity. Instead, he proposed that the Transitional Executive Council should exercise these powers.[51]

2.2.2 The Security Forces

For free and fair elections, the ability to campaign anywhere in the country is crucial. With the culture of intolerance widely shared in all sections of the community, and violence used as a political strategy, the security forces were bound to play an important role in either ensuring or restricting free political activity. The right to hold a meeting in a politically declared no-go area called for police protection.

The realities of South African political life placed the state security forces in a dominant position. Yet, these security forces had played a pivotal role in the construction, maintenance and continuation of the apartheid state. Their role in politics continued after 2 February 1990 despite protestations to the contrary. Their complicity in actions against the ANC is well documented.

The question, then, was who would control the police and the military during the election period? In line with the creation of a Transitional Executive Council, joint control of the armed forces was the obvious answer. At first it appeared as if the ANC would drop the demand for joint control of the armed forces and accept that the Transitional Executive Council sub-councils for defence and the police would perform only a supervisory role.[52] Joe Modise, the commander of Umkontho weSizwe, the military wing of the ANC, however,

---

50. *Weekly Mail* 23-29 July 1993.
51. *Ibid.*
52. Mac Maharaj, ANC negotiator, *Weekly Mail* 7-13 May 1993.

demanded joint control and insisted that the sub-council on defence take control of the Defence Force. This would mean that the sub-council would be able to intervene on all military issues which would affect the levelling of the political playing field.[53]

The same issues were raised with regard to the police. Peter Gastrow, Democratic Party MP, argued that there could be no free and fair election if the police remained under the sole control of the NP.[54] Hernus Kriel, Minister of Law and Order, rather lamely asserted that joint political control of the South African Police was unnecessary because the SAP served the whole country, not the NP.[55] On both the police and the SADF the Government remained intransigent and joint control of the armed forces remained a major obstacle.

The way out of the conflict appeared to be the creation of a national peace-keeping force, which would draw personnel from all armed formations and which would fall under multi-party control.[56] It would be involved in 'patrolling the streets of our towns, controlling crowds in a humane way, preventing disruption of political activity and protecting polling stations'.[57] The reason for this force was, in the words of Cyril Ramaphosa, that it 'will have the legitimacy and the credibility that is required to usher the country through the transition period'.[58] This proved be an expedient way of overcoming a major obstacle to the elections though the major problem of uniting the armed formations in South Africa remained unresolved.

2.2.3 The State-Controlled Media

In the past the Government used the state-controlled electronic media extensively and effectively in their election campaigns. Consequently the argument over the state domination of the airwaves had been in progress for some time.[59] At issue was the creation of a separate independent commission for the control of broadcasting and the

---

53. *Weekly Mail* 14-20 May 1993.
54. *Weekly Mail* 14-20 May 1993.
55. *Ibid.*
56. *Guardian Weekly* 23-29 July 1993.
57. Cyril Ramaphosa, *Weekly Mail* 23-29 July 1993.
58. *Weekly Mail* 23-29 July 1993.
59. Nogxina & Pikoli, above, n. 29, p. 10.

restructuring of the South African Broadcasting Corporation (SABC). A new board was appointed for the SABC in April 1993 after wide consultation and public hearings.[60] When President De Klerk interfered in the appointment of some members and the chairperson, the impartiality and legitimacy of the Board was again questioned.

2.3 Sovereignty and the International Community

Closely aligned to the question of election supervision was the role of the international community. For years the Government maintained that apartheid was a domestic issue which fell outside the domain of the international community. The transition from apartheid to democracy would likewise be a domestic affair in which the international community had no part to play.

The African National Congress, on the other hand, had been extremely successful in arguing the reverse and succeeded in making apartheid an international issue. Its demise, through the holding of the election, should consequently also be an international affair. To secure the successful transition to democracy, the international community had an important role to play, *inter alia*, as a member of the Independent Election Commission.

At issue was sovereignty and two competing views emerged. The De Klerk Government resisted international involvement doggedly because any involvement in the past meant a collision course with that community. The ANC, on the other hand, drew its strength from the international legal order in its campaign against apartheid, succeeding in getting apartheid declared a crime in international law.

Under pressure, the De Klerk Government reluctantly allowed international involvement. The first issue was the presence of international organisations to monitor the violence. A dispute followed over their appellation: were they to be called monitors or observers? The former name evoked greater involvement than the latter. Thus the UN, the Commonwealth and the Organisation of African Unity were accorded the status of 'observers'.

For the issue to be resolved the concept of sovereignty must first be negotiated. Would it be the narrow exclusive definition that the

---

60. *Cape Argus* 27 May 1993.

apartheid state adopted or a broader international view which holds that sovereignty is bounded by international norms and obligations. The definition was not only relevant to the immediate question of international election supervision, but also to South Africa's future relations with the international community and the acceptance of the norms and standards of the international legal order. Being a fully-fledged member of this community is incompatible with an exclusive definition of sovereignty; the international legal order imposes a diminution of national sovereignty, an implication that the apartheid regime had resisted, to no avail, for the past four decades.

3 NEGOTIATED DEMOCRACY

For a democratic state to emerge in South Africa fundamental issues have to be resolved. What is the South African state? What are the limitations on state sovereignty? How can legitimate state authorities be created? Underlying much of these issues are conflicting views of and approaches to democracy.

The problem of arriving at a common understanding of democracy derives from the fact that the competing conceptions of democracy are embedded in the real world of political power. Theories of democracy do not necessarily give direction or form to the debate. Arguments are interest based rather than principle based. Evidence for this view is to be found in the language used by the political players and in what they do and often do not do. With a minority-support base, the primary interests of the NP and IFP (and other Homeland governments) are inevitably to underplay the majoritarian principle of democracy. Even the ANC approach to democracy was not divorced from constituency politics. In facing the question of whether there should be a threshold percentage for representation in the constituent assembly, Penuel Maduna, an ANC Constitutional Committee member, located the question primarily in terms of partisan interests. He wrote that a discussion of the issue

> will have to be informed by numerous factors, *inter alia*, the interests of the ANC and the entire Revolutionary Alliance, the relations the ANC has with the broader democratic forces, the interests of the Patriotic Front, as well as the

political balance of forces within the South African political spectrum.[61]

How the conflict of partisan interests would be resolved was dependent, in the end, on the last consideration—'the political balance of forces within the South African political spectrum'. The ANC was very sanguine about the creation of laws. Zola Skweyiya, the chairperson of the ANC Constitutional Committee, observed that 'All laws, electoral laws not excepted, do not operate in abstract but in concrete historical contexts'.[62] He concluded that 'in the final analysis, it is the conditions that obtain in this country, which will define the content of our electoral regime'.[63] Through the process of negotiations a peculiarly South African content will be given to the concept of democracy.

Democracy cannot, however, assume any meaning which the most powerful force in a society wishes to impress on the concept. Placing 'Democratic' in the name of the former East Germany did not make the DDR democratic. Claiming that the one-party state in Africa was democratic in terms of some African notion of democracy did not in the end wash with the electorate. Democracy is not simply a matter of attaching a name to a process, and then expecting that the desired consequences of the idealised notion of democracy will follow. A constituent assembly elected, but with no authentic powers, will simply not rise by the coat tails of the word democracy, however many times it is chanted in the official media. The democratic process is not an end in itself but a process whereby a durable state authority is created. Legitimacy is the consequence of democratic elections; it is earned, not accorded to an institution. The negotiated content of democracy should therefore not undermine the very purpose of the transition process—the creation of a legitimate state.

The negotiated concepts of democracy will reflect the dynamics of politics as seen by the parties in the light of the forthcoming election. It will, however, also have long-term implications. A constitution which is agreed upon without substantive support from the majority, will soon crack under the strain of its own lack of legitimacy no matter how

---

61. Maduna, above, n. 31, p. 22.
62. `Forward' in Centre for Development Studies, *Electoral Laws in Transitional Arrangements* (1993) 2.
63. *Ibid.*

carefully it has been legally entrenched. Moreover, anti-democratic elements may become part of the fabric of the future political institutions. The type of rules which will be negotiated may well survive the first election and become institutionalised in the new legal order. It is therefore important that if the long-term success of democracy is to be ensured, the short-term agreements are not totally divorced from ideal notions of democracy.

Chapter Four

A Bill of Rights as an Instrument for Social and Economic Transformation in a New South African Constitution: Lessons from India

Pierre de Vos

1 INTRODUCTION

It is common cause that a new South African constitution, negotiated by a constituent assembly, will contain a justiciable Bill of Rights and a specifically stated commitment to social change. All the major political groupings in the country represented at the Conference for a Democratic South Africa (CODESA) agreed to this premise in late 1991.[1] There is still considerable difference of opinion, however, on

---

1. The first meeting of CODESA on December 20, 1991 was attended by 19 political groupings, which included the representatives of all 10 of the so-called Homelands and the major political parties represented in Parliament. Two important groupings voluntarily excluded themselves from this process—the Pan Africanist Congress (PAC) on the far left of the political spectrum, and the white right, represented by the Conservative Party (CP). The CODESA talks were suspended after the Boipatong massacre in May 1992, but bilateral talks between the government and other parties were resumed. At the end of 1992, President F.W. De Klerk announced a time schedule for transition in which he envisaged the formal resumption of multiparty negotiations by April 1993. These negotiations had as their aim to establish the structures for an interim government, with the view to having a free and fair election for an interim government by April 1994. The new interim government also would function as a constituent assembly and would

Negotiating Justice

the contents of such a Bill of Rights. One of the major areas of controversy centres around the possible incorporation, formulation and ultimate enforcement of social and economic rights in such a Bill of Rights. Although most parties agree on the necessity to include at least some social and economic rights in one form or another in a Bill of Rights, the general commitment of most parties to the social transformation of society seems at best tenuous. This is in sharp contrast to the view which has taken hold among the poor and disenfranchised sections of the community, that a Bill of Rights, crammed with all the important social and economic rights, will play a major role in the social and economic transformation of South African society.

In this chapter I pose the question how a South African Bill of Rights could best be formulated to try and satisfy the, sometimes unrealistic, expectations of the vast majority of the population. Can the legal system in general, and a judicially enforceable Bill of Rights in particular, address the social and economic problems of the country in an effective way? In other words, can such a Bill of Rights—even if it includes so called second and third generation rights—assist in transforming the social reality in which most South Africans find themselves today.

In an attempt to answer these questions, I will look at the Indian constitutional jurisprudence of the past 40 years. The incorporation of a set of directive principles in a separate Part of the Indian Bill of Rights, and the judicial response to this, will be analysed. Drawing from the Indian experience, I will propose a specific formulation which, in my opinion, would assist in establishing a Bill of Rights as a document with at least marginal relevance to the lives of the citizens of this country. In this regard, I warn that the mechanisms through which the Bill of Rights will 'come alive' should be clearly formulated in the constitution. The very real temptation of shying away from such a task

---

draw up a new constitution which would include a justiciable Bill of Rights. *See* Phillipa Garson, 'The trigger fingers are twitching - will we make their day?', *Weekly Mail* January 8-14 1993; Frederik Van Zyl Slabbert, 'Die ABC van die oorgang na demokrasie' ('The ABC of the transition to democracy'), *Die Suid-Afrikaan* no. 43 (February/March 1993), pp. 4 to 8; and Gavin Evans & Paul Strober 'African National Congress moderates win the day', *Weekly Mail* February 19-25.

A Bill of Rights: Lessons from India

in order to facilitate compromise, should, I believe, be avoided at all cost.

2 FUNDAMENTAL RIGHTS AND DIRECTIVE PRINCIPLES IN THE INDIAN CONSTITUTION

Members of the constituent assembly, who were charged with the task of drafting a new Indian constitution, decided to set out the 'fundamental rights' in Part III of the document. These rights included all the traditional civil and political rights such as the right to freedom of speech and assembly, the right to (formal) equality and the right to a fair trial. The rights in Part III of the constitution were made subject to judicial review and the State was prohibited from making any law which 'takes away or abridges the rights conferred' in Part III.[2] The legislature was, however, empowered to amend the constitution—including the fundamental rights in Part III—in any way it chose.[3]

Members of the constituent assembly stated at the time of independence that it was their aim to draft a constitution which would facilitate a complete social transformation of society.[4] The constituent assembly therefore decided to include social and economic rights in the constitution. These rights were formulated as unenforceable directive principles and incorporated separately in Part IV of the constitution. In a delicate compromise between pragmatists and idealists in the constituent assembly, the directive principles—which were included in Part IV—were made unenforceable, but the principles therein laid down were nevertheless described as 'fundamental for the governance of the country'. The State was also charged with the duty to apply these principles in making laws.[5] The constituent assembly had great

---

2. Article 13(2).
3. Article 13, Article 32 and Article 226.
4. '[The] utility of the State has to be judged from its effect on the common man's welfare, and that the constitution must establish the State's obligation beyond doubt.' Per H.V. Kamath, *Constituent Assemblies Debates (CAD)* VII 2 221 (New Delhi).
5. Article 37 states: 'The provisions contained in this Part shall not be enforceable by any court, but the principles therein laid down are nevertheless fundamental in the governance of the country and it shall be the duty of the State to apply these principles in making law.'

difficulty in achieving consensus on the phrasing and the application of certain sections of Part III and Part IV of the constitution, and the decision to 'relegate' social and economic rights to unenforceable principles was 'severely criticised by some delegates'.[6]

In the end the directive principles were formulated in a rather vague way and it was not made clear how the court should deal with a situation where a direct clash between the directive principles and fundamental rights occurred. It was also not made clear whether the Parliament would have the power to amend the fundamental rights whenever those rights thwarted the attainment of the principles set out in Part IV. It took the Indian Supreme Court more than 30 years to come to grips with this matter, its view veering wildly from one extreme to the other. Almost the only principle to which the court stuck through all these years was that the directive principles could not be enforced directly by the courts; in other words, that the directive principles and fundamental rights did not give powers to the legislature and the executive that it otherwise would not have had.

In any attempt to systemise and understand the Indian constitutional jurisprudence of the past 45 years, it must be realised that the courts view of the relationship between the fundamental rights in Part III and the directive principles in Part IV, were shaped by two distinct constitutional questions:

▼ Firstly, questions about the interaction between directive principles and fundamental rights came into play directly where the State, through legislative or executive action, attempted to implement directive principles and in the process infringed upon, or restricted, the fundamental rights set out in Part III. The courts then had to decide whether the fundamental rights had preeminence over legislation or executive acts purportedly adopted to realise the goals set out in the directive principles.

▼ Secondly, questions about the interaction between directive principles and fundamental rights came into play where the court had to decide about the status of the fundamental rights; in other words

---

6. Delegate T.T. Krishnamarachi described the principles as 'a veritable dustbin of sentiment [...] sufficiently resilient as to permit any individual of this House to ride his hobby horse into it' CAD 1949 Vol. VII 41-42. See further CAD 1949, Vol. VII no 2 225-583 for the complete debate where the directive principles are variously described as 'platitudes' and 'pious wishes' on the one hand, and as 'the essence of the constitution' on the other.

A Bill of Rights: Lessons from India

whether they were in some way 'higher law' or whether they could be amended through any whim of Parliament. These questions were specifically pertinent where the court had to decide whether the fundamental rights, which stood in the way of the realisation of directive principles, could be amended by the legislature or not.

In an attempt to make some sense of the approach taken by the Indian Supreme Court, the court's attitude towards these questions can be divided into three phases.

2.1 The First Phase: Independence to 1960

2.1.1 Clash Between Directive Principles and Fundamental Rights

Where a law was enacted to give effect to one of the directive principles and it came into direct conflict with one of the fundamental rights, the courts gave precedence to the fundamental rights and declared the legislation invalid.[7] However, fundamental rights were only given this position of primacy when attempts to harmonise the offending law with the right set out in Part III failed.

This approach can be well demonstrated by the decision in the case of *Mohammed Hanif Quareshi* v. *State of Bihar*.[8] *In casu* the validity of the Bihar Preservation and Improvement of Animals Act (2 of 1956), which prohibited the slaughtering of cows and calves, was contested. The offending law constituted an attempt to give effect to Article 48 of the directive principles.[9] A group of butchers contested the validity of this law, claiming that it contravened their fundamental right to conduct a business, which is guaranteed as a fundamental right

---

7. *State of Madras* v. *Champakam Dorairajan* (1951) SCR 525, 531; ('51) ASC 266. Das J. remarked: 'The Chapter on fundamental rights is sacrosanct and not liable to be abridged by the legislator or the executive act or order except to the extent provided by appropriate articles in Part III. The Directive Principles [...] have to conform and run subsidiary to the Chapter on Fundamental Rights.' (531).
8. (1959) SCR 629, ('58) ASC 73.
9. Article 48: 'The State shall endeavour to organise agriculture and animal husbandry on modern and scientific lines and shall, in particular, take steps for preserving and improving the breeds, and prohibiting the slaughter, of cows and calves and other milk and draught cattle.'

in Article 19(1)(g) of the constitution.[10]

The court reiterated its position that no law may infringe upon the fundamental rights in Part III of the constitution, not even when it constituted an attempt to give effect to goals set out in one of the directive principles. The court stressed, however, that a harmonious interpretation must be followed. The State must implement the directive principles, but in such a way that it does not take away or abridge the fundamental rights in any way in the process.[11] *In casu* the court found that the law did not infringe upon the fundamental rights. No right is absolute. Reasonable restrictions on fundamental rights are necessary and acceptable. The law under discussion contained an extensive classification of the animals that may or may not be slaughtered; this classification was reasonable and there was therefore no infringement of equality before the law.[12]

2.1.2 The Status of Fundamental Rights

The Supreme Court's insistence in the first ten years after independence that fundamental rights have preference over directive principles when there is a direct clash between them, did not in any way mean that the court saw the constitution—or even the fundamental rights—as supreme. The court made it clear from the start that Parliament could amend the fundamental rights to facilitate the realisation of the goals set out in the directive principles. The court was of the opinion that fundamental rights were more important than directive principles, but stressed that the constitution had empowered the legislature to amend the fundamental rights to ensure that these rights did not impede the attainment of the directive principles.

---

10. (1959) SCR 655. Article 19(1) states: 'All citizens shall have the right ... (g) to practice any profession, or to carry on any occupation, trade or business.'
11. Above, n. 8, p. 638.
12. Above, n. 8, p. 733-734. For further commentary on the case *cf.* Seervai H. M., (1983) *Indian Constitution II* 3rd ed., (Tripathi, Bombay), 1581; Pandey J. N., *Constitutional Law of India* 20th ed.; (Central Law Agency, 1989, Allahabad) p. 254; and Hasan S. *Supreme Court: Fundamental Rights and Directive Principles* 2nd ed.. (Deep & Deep Publications, 1984, New Delhi), p. 55. Hasan is of the opinion that the case 'tilts the Supreme Court towards the directive principles'.

A Bill of Rights: Lessons from India

Soon after the adoption of the constitution it became clear that most legislation providing for the expropriation of land would contravene the fundamental right to property protected in Article 19(1)(f) of the constitution. The Government, which was committed to a programme of land reform, promptly amended the right to property to ensure the constitutionality of its expropriation laws. These amendments were then unsuccessfully challenged in the Supreme Court.[13] The Supreme Court therefore allowed for the watering down of the property clause because it did not want to infringe upon the power of Parliament to implement the directive principles.

2.2 The Second Phase: 1960 to 1977

2.2.1 Clash Between Fundamental Rights and Directive Principles

The different decisions of the Supreme Court during this phase are difficult to reconcile. Where the status of the fundamental rights were in issue, the court blocked the amendment of the fundamental rights—even where amendments were necessary to give effect to the directive principles. But where a clash occurred between the fundamental rights on the one hand, and legislation purporting to give effect to the directive principles on the other, the court took a more conciliatory approach in which it viewed these as supplementary to each other. It therefore attempted to interpret the fundamental rights *within* the contexts of the directive principles.

The development of this trend culminated in the decision of *Chandra Bhavan Boarding and Lodging Bangalore v. Mysore*.[14] The validity of certain provisions of the Minimum Wage Act of 1948 was challenged by the applicants on the grounds that it infringed the fundamental right to equality, guaranteed in Article 14 of the constitution. The applicants also claimed that the provisions of the Act, which empowered the Government to arbitrarily set minimum wages, infringed upon their right to carry on any trade or business. The court rejected this argument and ruled that the legislation was valid. The

---

13. *Shankari Prasad Singh Deo* v. *Union of India* AIR 38 (1951) SC 458; (1952) SCR 89.
14. (1970) 2 SCR 600; (1970) ASC 2042.

court stated that the fundamental rights in Part III could not be seen in isolation.

> Provisions of the Constitution are not erected as the barrier of progress. They provide a plan for the orderly progress towards a social order contemplated by the preamble of the Constitution [...] While the rights conferred by Part III are fundamental the Directive Principles given under Part IV are fundamental in the governance of the country. We see *no conflict on the whole between the provisions contained in Part III and Part IV*. They are complementary and supplementary to each other. The provisions in Part IV enable the legislators and the government to impose various duties on citizens. The provisions therein are deliberately made elastic because the duties to be imposed on citizens depend on the extent to which the Directive Principles are implemented.[15]

The court thus attempted to reconcile the fundamental rights and the directive principles as far as possible. In doing so, the court began to interpret the fundamental rights within the context of the constitution as a whole and specifically took cognizance of the social goals set out in the directive principles.

2.3 Status of Fundamental Rights

Despite the court's more accommodating approach to the relationship between fundamental rights and directive principles, it took a more restricted view of the power of the legislature to amend the constitution, even where this was done in order to remove obstacles in the way of the implementation of the directive principles. In the process it made important pronouncements on the relationship between fundamental rights and directive principles.

The Supreme Court shook the legal and political world in India when it handed down the decision in the case of *I.C. Golaknath* v. *State of Punjab*.[16] *In casu* the court had to decide on the validity of amendments to the fundamental right to property. These amendments constituted an attempt to water down the fundamental right to property

---

15. (1970) ASC 2050.
16. AIR (54) 1967 SC 1643; (1967) 2 SCR 762.

A Bill of Rights: Lessons from India

by excluding judicial review of legislation or executive action allowing for the expropriation of property. The court declared the amendment invalid, pronouncing the fundamental rights to be sacrosanct. It held that the fundamental rights in Part III of the constitution could never be changed by the legislature. It then proceeded to indicate what the relationship between these dominant provisions and the less important directive principles might be.[17] The court argued that Parts III and IV of the constitution set up an 'integrated scheme forming a self contained code'.[18] The fundamental rights should be interpreted in the light of the goals and ideals set out in the directive principles. There was, in fact, no clash between the fundamental rights and the directive principles, because the scheme was so elastic that all the directives could be implemented without restriction of the fundamental rights. The constitution itself provided for the suspension or derogation of fundamental rights in specific circumstances.[19] In deciding on whether such circumstances existed, the courts must also take into account the content of the directive principles. However, where the constitution does not provide for the derogation or restriction of fundamental rights, the parliament can never restrict or abolish fundamental rights at will.

This case created a huge outcry in India. Some lawyers praised the decision as a show of judicial statesmanship,[20] while others voiced the opinion that the decision would severely hamper the realisation of social and economic rights.[21] A more moderate approach regarding the

---

17. Aikman C.C. 'The Debate on the Amendment of the Indian Constitution *Victoria University Law Review* (1978) pp. 357-369.
18. AIR (54) 1967 SC 1656; (1967) 2 SCR 789.
19. AIR (54) 1967 SC 1656; (1967) 2 SCR 789. *Cf* Aikman C.C., *Victoria University Law Review* (1978) p. 369.
20. Imam M. *The Indian Supreme Court and the Constitution* (New Delhi, 1968), p. 8: '[A] demonstration of judicial statesmanship of a rare vintage, a culmination of a long trend in judicial process.'
21. Ray A., Chatterjee S. K. & Venkatasubbiah V. *Political Development and Constitutional Change* (Vikas Publishing House, 1982 New Delhi), p. 44: 'The court through its decision in the *Golaknath* case had stood in the way of the implementation of the directive principles, and its impact resulted in the sharp articulation of divisions in India's political system. In other words, the implications of the *Golaknath* case was that even if the fundamental rights were a fetter on social and economic change as desired by the people, the elected representatives of the people could not move in until the court reversed its ruling.' *Cf.* generally, Sood P., *Politics of Socio-economic Change in India* (Marwah Publications, 1979, New Delhi) p. 41.

status of fundamental rights in the constitution came to the fore in the monumental case of *Kesavananda Bharti* v. *Union of India*.[22] In this case, dealing with a challenge to the constitution (Twenty-fifth Amendment) Act of 1971, a majority of the court declined to agree with the judges in the *Golaknath* case that fundamental rights could never be amended by the legislature. The Supreme Court took a compromise position and declared that the amendment powers of the legislature—which admittedly were very wide—were nevertheless restricted in that the *basic structure or framework* of the constitution could never be changed or amended in any way. The court attempted to find a balance between the view that there should be no restriction on the power of the legislature to amend the constitution on the one hand, and the view that the constitution, as higher law, should be beyond the reach of Parliament on the other. In doing so, the court reiterated its view that, in principle, there was no clash between the fundamental rights and the directive principles.[23] The fundamental rights and directive principles actually supported each other because they were aimed at achieving the same goals, namely the social revolution and the achieving of a welfare state, as envisaged by the constitution.[24]

---

22. AIR (60) 1973 SC 1461; 1973 Supp. SCR. The case is also known as the 'Fundamental Rights Case'. Eleven decisions were handed down and were printed in a 998 page special supplement to the law reports.
23. AIR 73 SC 1461. Shelat J. and Grover J.: 'Both Parts III and IV have to be balanced and harmonised' (1582); Hedge J. and Mukherjee J.: '[T]here is no antithesis between fundamental rights and directive principles. The directive principles lay down the end to be achieved and part III prescribes the means through which the goal is to be reached' (1641).
24. Pandey J. N., *Constitutional Law of India* 246; and Hasan S., *Supreme Court* 56. *Cf. Marsar Manghani* v. *Sangram Sampat* AIR 1960 Punjab 35 40 ('Directive Principles is part of the constitution which is one organic whole...'; and *Pratap R & T Factory* v. *State of Punjab* AIR 1966 Punjab 16 20 ('[directive principles are] an important and integral part of our constitution').

A Bill of Rights: Lessons from India

2.4 The Third Phase: 1978 to the Present

2.4.1 Clash Between Fundamental Rights and Directive Principles

During the state of emergency, which was instituted at the end of Indira Gandhi's first period in office, the Supreme Court sanctioned the most gross violations and abuses of power by the State. But within a few months after the end of the state of emergency the court flowered as a champion of the rights of the poor and destitute people of India. Judges began to view themselves as participants in the political process and saw the handing down of judicial decisions as political happenings which were directly related to the social well-being of the people.[25] The court's new approach, in which it saw constitutional interpretation not as something mechanical but as part of a bigger process, contributed to the rise in importance of the directive principles. Fundamental rights were now being interpreted within the context of the social and political ethos of the constitution as a whole.

The Supreme Court developed this holistic approach in cases where it had to determine the validity of legislation in the light of the 25th Amendment which incorporated Article 31C into the constitution. This Article stated that any law made to give effect to the principles laid out in Article 39(b) and (c),[26] could not be invalidated by any court. Legislation which attempted to give effect to these principles would be valid even when it clashed directly with one of the fundamental rights. In cases where such legislation was challenged, the Supreme Court approached the question by looking at the constitution as a whole. This new approach was well illustrated by the case of *State of Tamil Nadu* v. *L. Abu Kavur Bai*.[27] In this case the Supreme Court had to decide upon the validity of the Tamil Nadu Stage Carriage (Acquisition) Act 12 of 1973, which authorised the State to nationalise stage carriages. The court, per Fazal Ali J., declared the legislation valid[28] because it had

---

25. Ghouse 'Constitutional Law I' in *Annual Survey of Indian Law* (1978) 393.
26. Article 39 - The State shall, in particular, direct its policy towards securing-
    (b) that the ownership and control of the material resources of the community are so distributed as best to subserve the common good.
    (c) that the operation of the economic system does not result in the concentration of wealth and means of production to the common detriment.
27. A.I.R (71) (1984) SC 326; SCR 1984 (1) 725.
28. Above, n. 27, p. 366A.

been adopted to implement the directive principles, set out in Article 39(b) and (c).[29] Fazal Ali J. stressed that Article 31C required a strong nexus between the legislation and the directive principles before such legislation (*prima facie* contravening one of the fundamental rights) could be found by the court to be valid.[30] The fact that legislation contained a declaration to the effect that it was adopted to further one of the directive principles could be used as evidence that a reasonable link between the Act and the principle did in fact exist.[31] A scheme of nationalisation aimed at redistribution of wealth, such as in the present case, showed a requisite nexus to acquire the protection of Article 31C.[32]

The court's position was therefore as follows: where there was a direct clash between legislation adopted in an attempt to realise one of the goals set out in the directive principles, and a fundamental right in Part III, the court would first have to determine whether the legislation was aimed at achieving the goals set out in Article 39(b) or (c). If it was, the legislation would be valid. If not, the court would first attempt to reconcile the legislation and the fundamental right in question. In the process of reconciliation, the courts came up with innovative interpretations which, in fact, blurred the strict boundaries between fundamental rights and directive principles.

2.5 Status of Fundamental Rights

The question about the status of the constitution—and the fundamental rights in particular—was finally resolved in two very important cases where the court had to decide on the validity of the constitution (Forty-second Amendment) Act of 1976. The Act constituted an attempt by Parliament to circumvent the 'basic structure' principle devised by the court in the *Kesavananda Bharti* case. To do this, the amendment prohibited *all* judicial review of constitutional amendments by adding two sub-clauses to Article 368. Article 368 generally allowed for the

---

29. Above, n. 27, p. 739F-740A.
30. Above, n. 27, p. 739G.
31. Above, n. 27, p. 739H-740A.
32. Above, n. 27, p. 764B-C.

A Bill of Rights: Lessons from India

amendment of the constitution.[33] The first important case in which the validity of these amendments came before the court, was that of *Minerva Mills Ltd.* v. *Union of India*,[34] in which the court invalidated the inclusion of sub-clauses 4 and 5 in Article 368. The court was of the opinion that these sub-clauses were invalid because they destroyed the basic structure of the constitution. 'The power to destroy,' said Chandrachud CJ., 'is not the power to amend'.[35]

In coming to this conclusion the chief justice discussed the relationship between Parts III and IV of the constitution. According to him, these two Parts were the core elements which operated as the conscience of the constitution.[36] Directive principles were fundamental in the governance of the country. But if the guarantees in Part III were destroyed in an attempt to give effect to the principles in Part IV, the basic structure of the constitution would also be destroyed.[37] The Indian constitution was built on the foundation of a balance between the directive principles and fundamental rights. To give absolute precedence to one or the other would destroy the harmony of the constitution.[38] The fundamental rights set out in Part III of the constitution were not ends in themselves. The end was set out by Part IV. That was why the rights guaranteed in Part III were subject to reasonable restrictions.[39]

> The goals set out in Part IV have, therefore, to be achieved without the abrogation of the means provided for by Part III [...] Anything that destroys the balance between the two Parts will *ipso facto* destroy an essential element of the basic structure of the Constitution. Granville Austin's observation

---

33. These subclauses stated:
    '(4) No amendment of this constitution (including the provisions of part III) made or purporting to have been made under this article [...] shall be called into question in any court on any ground.
    '(5) For the removal of doubts, it is hereby declared that there shall be no limitation whatever on the constituent power of parliament to amend by way of addition, variation or repeal the provisions of the constitution under this article.'
34. AIR (1980) 67; SCR (1980) 1 206.
35. Above, n. 34, p. 240C-E
36. Above, n. 34, p. 253D-H, 256A-B.
37. Above, n. 34, p. 254H.
38. Above, n. 34, p. 355C-D.
39. Above, n. 34, p. 253D-H.

> brings out the true position that Parts III and IV are like two wheels of a chariot, one no less important than the other. You snap one and the other will lose its efficacy. [...] The Indian Constitution is founded on the bedrock of the balance between Parts III and IV. To give absolute primacy to one over the other is to disturb the harmony of the Constitution. This harmony and balance between fundamental rights and directive principles is an essential feature of the basic structure of the Constitution.[40]

The *Minerva Mills* decision made clear that the status of the fundamental rights could not be seen in isolation because it was not an end in itself. It was only the means whereby the aims set out in Part IV could be realised. The judgment created a subtle balance between the fundamental rights in Part III and the directive principles in Part IV, whereby the potential for a creative and symbiotic relationship between these different sections was opened up.

This principle was further refined in the case of *Waman Rao* v. *Union of India*.[41] In this case, the court stressed that directive principles were in no way inferior or subordinate to fundamental rights and in the process it shifted the emphasis in the application of the basic structure doctrine. In the previous cases the basic structure doctrine was used by the courts to invalidate legislation which infringed upon the fundamental rights, and this created the impression that at least the majority of fundamental rights formed part of the basic structure of the constitution. In *Waman Rao* the court emphasised that the constitution was a document of social and economic upliftment. Any law which constituted a *bona fide* attempt to give effect to this basic goal of the constitution would augment the basic structure of the constitution even where, on the face of it, it infringed upon the fundamental rights. In other words, the court said that where legislation was adopted to give effect to the directive principles, it would be valid unless it destroyed the balance between the fundamental rights and the directive principles.

The reason for this shift of emphasis was highlighted by the separate decision of Bhagwati J. in which he sketched the problems with which the court was faced in deciding these issues.

---

40. Above, n. 34, p. 256A-B. The references to Granville Austin are from the book *The Indian Constitution: Cornerstone of a Nation* (Bombay, 1972).
41. A.I.R 68 (1981) SC 271.

A Bill of Rights: Lessons from India

> There were millions of people in the country who were steeped in poverty and destitution and for them, civil and political rights had no meaning. It was realised that to the large majority of people who are living an almost sub-human existence in conditions of abject poverty and for whom life is one long unbroken story of want and destitution, notions of individual freedom and liberty, though representing some of the most cherished values of free society, would sound as empty words bandied about only in the drawing rooms of the rich and well-to-do.[42]

The Indian constitution, declared Judge Bhagwati, was a social document. Despite the fact that fundamental rights were important for democracy, there could be no real democracy where there was no real attempt to reach the goal of social and economic justice for all in society.

> [T]o create socio-economic conditions in which there can be social and political justice to everyone, is the theme of the directive principles. It is the directive principles which nourish the roots of our democracy, provide strength and vigour to it and attempt to make it a real participatory democracy which does not remain merely a political democracy but also becomes social and economic democracy with fundamental rights available to all irrespective of their power, position or wealth. The dynamic provisions fertilise the static provisions of the fundamental rights.[43]

3 THE CONSTITUTIONAL EFFECT OF DIRECTIVE PRINCIPLES

The decisions in the *Minerva Mills* and *Waman Rao* cases, in which the Supreme Court stressed the interdependent nature of the fundamental rights and the directive principles, had a tremendous impact on the influence of the directive principle in every aspect of the Indian constitutional system. During the 1980s, consecutive Indian governments—implicitly accepting the notion that there will always be an inherent clash between high economic growth and the implementation of social and economic rights—chose to pursue policies

---

42. Above, n. 41, para. 103.
43. Above, n. 41, para. 107.

that would yield high economic growth. The Supreme Court stepped into the void as ally of the marginalised sectors of the community through its innovative interpretation of the symbiotic relationship between the directive principles and the fundamental rights.

3.1 The Interpretation of Fundamental Rights in the Constitution

In the previous section it was pointed out that the Supreme Court authoritatively stated in the early 1980s that neither fundamental rights nor directive principles should have precedence over the other.[44] This must not be seen as an attempt by the court to resolve the tension between the fundamental rights (and the individual interest protected by them) on the one hand, and the directive principles (and the interest of social and economic justice they may protect or advance) on the other. On the contrary, the court sought to channel this tension in a creative way to flesh out and give substance to both kinds of rights.

In the recent past, the courts have stressed the importance of keeping a *balance* between the fundamental rights and the directive principles. The judges do this by looking at the milieu out of which the constitution was born, and by interpreting the different provisions in Part III of the constitution in the light of this. In doing so, the judges always take into account the principles set out in Part IV of the constitution. The traditional fundamental rights are thus infused with a completely new social and economic meaning. The directive principles now operate as supporting (legal) norms, thus imbuing the fundamental rights with new content and substance. In using this method, the right to equality, for example, acquires a much wider meaning when read within the context of the directive principles. Now the right to equality does not only mean the right to formal equality, but the right—given the goal of substantive equality set out in the directive principles—to be treated equally. The right to equality is now placed in a social context. The possibility of individual rights obstructing the realisation of social and economic rights is now mitigated because the individual rights are imbued with social and economic content. This forces even the most conservative and positivist-minded judge to take note of social and

---

44. In *Minerva Mills Ltd* v. *Union of India* A.I.R. *(1980) 67; SCR (1980) 1 206;* and *Waman Rao* v. *Union of India* A.I.R 68 (1981) SC 271. *Cf supra* 5 3 2.

A Bill of Rights: Lessons from India

economic realities in interpreting the fundamental rights. The courts can now read directive principles into fundamental rights, thus 'discovering new rights' in situations where this was not explicitly prohibited by the legislature.[45] Thus, the goals set out in the directive principles can even in some case be enforced via the fundamental rights.

An example of this principle can be found in the case of *Akhil Bharatiya Soshit Karamchari Sang (Railway)* v. *Union of India and others*.[46] In this case regulations which allocated a certain percentage of positions in the railway administration for scheduled castes and tribes and allowed for other forms of affirmative action, was challenged by the applicants on the ground that it contravened the equality principle set out in Articles 14 and 16 in Part III of the constitution. The State opposed this challenge on the ground that Article 46 in the directive principles ordered the State to promote the educational and economic interest of scheduled castes and tribes. The majority of the court, per Chinnappa Reddy and Krishna JJ., agreed that no infringement took place. Both decisions emphasised that the court must take into account the social milieu—which gives the constitution a living meaning. The courts must try to understand the people for whom the constitution was made; must try to understand their frustrations, the finer ethos, their aspirations, and the parameters set down by the constitution for the solving of the socio-economic problems.[47] In interpreting the constitution, the court must not get stuck at the words alone, but must also take into account the philosophy and the spirit behind the constitution.[48] This philosophy and spirit is closely related to the goals set out in Part IV of the constitution.

In casu the court rejected the challenge. The court declared that the classification of the population will not necessarily infringe on the rights set out in Articles 14 and 16. On the contrary, because of the huge gap between scheduled castes and tribes on the one hand, and the rest of the population on the other, the fundamental right to equality—in the light of the provision of Article 46—should be read as a *justification* of the categorisation of scheduled castes and tribes. The

---

45. Sathe, S. P. 'Constitutional Law I' 222 in Jaccob R (ed.) *Annual Survey of Indian Law* (1987, New Delhi).
46. (1981) 1 SCC 246.
47. Above, n. 46, p. 264 para. 23 *per* Krishna J.
48. Above, n. 46, p. 308 para. 122 *per* Chinnappa Reddy.

regulations were issued to strive towards the goal set out in Article 16 and 46 and were therefore valid.[49] In *Akhil Bharatiya* the court 'discovered' the right to affirmative action in the right to equality. The content and substance of the fundamental rights, set out in Articles 14, 16 and 21, are now enhanced and developed by the normative support of the directive principles.

4 THE INFLUENCE OF DIRECTIVE PRINCIPLES ON INDIAN JURISPRUDENCE

The influence of directive principles on Indian constitutional jurisprudence is much greater than is generally understood. Since the early 1980s almost all judicial decisions dealing with fundamental rights must also refer to the directive principles. The directive principles assist the court in determining exactly where the boundaries of the fundamental rights are, and whether restrictions on fundamental rights by the legislator or the executive are reasonable. Directive principles also play an important role where the courts have to interpret other legislation. The directive principles also operate as supporting legal norms and therefore supplement the substance of the fundamental rights. In the process the Supreme Court has 'discovered' new rights not explicitly guaranteed in Part III of the constitution. These include:
▼ the right to equal pay for equal work;
▼ the right of substantive equality;
▼ the right to livelihood;
▼ the right—in restricted cases—to the means to guarantee livelihood; and
▼ the right to a healthy environment.

The courts have also handed down some unorthodox orders to ensure that these rights are realised. The courts have been prepared to:
▼ order government institutions to take positive action to ensure that these institutions effectively fulfil their constitutional duty;
▼ issue judicial legislation to attain the same goal; and
▼ in restricted situations, to enforce these rights against third parties.

---

49. Above, n. 46, pp. 286-289.

A Bill of Rights: Lessons from India

In every case where the courts are called upon to interpret fundamental rights they will look at the principles laid down in Part IV of the constitution, and will make the order—where at all possible—which would give the biggest social and economic relief to the applicants.

This approach is not beyond criticism. In the process of opening up the fundamental rights, the principle of judicial interpretation has been followed which is context specific in the extreme. This resulted in making every new case wholly unpredictable. It thus became unclear which decisions could be relied on as precedents for following cases. The system of precedent as a whole became endangered and this was severely criticised.[50]

> [T]o take suffering seriously one must take the law making enterprise seriously too. In the absence of this, judgments become decree by *fiat*, they become remedies for specific events, not precedent for general application. [I]t makes justice seeking a subjective enterprise dependent upon the judge.

The result of this approach was that the court's innovative decisions did not always succeed in empowering groups not before the court. The decisions seldom had a long-term effect on the practices of government. It therefore remains an open question to what extent the court assisted in improving the living standards of the poor masses. This situation created the real danger that the courts could become merely another channel through which political pressure could be exercised on the powers that be. The poor sections of the community without access to the courts, who do not evoke the pity of the public interest lawyers, could then be forgotten.

5 PROBLEM AREAS IN THE RELATIONSHIP BETWEEN FUNDAMENTAL RIGHTS AND DIRECTIVE PRINCIPLES

The delegates who drafted the Indian constitution could never have predicted that the incorporation of enforceable fundamental rights and non-enforceable directive principles would have had such a turbulent

---

50. Singh C., 'Right to Life: Legal Activism or Legal Escapism?' *Journal of Indian Law Institute* vol. 28, no. 2 (1986), pp. 249-251.

but decisive influence on the legislature, executive and judiciary. This was despite the fact that unsatisfactory constitutional compromises were struck by the constituent assembly which ensured that certain core aspects of the constitution were left unresolved. Three aspects of the constitution can be highlighted in this regard.

▼ The drafters of the Indian constitution failed clearly to indicate what status the constitution in general, and the fundamental rights specifically, have. The original Article 368 empowered the legislature to amend the constitution—thus also the fundamental rights—in the prescribed manner. This created the impression that the constitution, with the exception of certain entrenched provisions, did not establish any higher law. On the other hand Article 13 stated that any law infringing on the fundamental rights would be invalid. This provision created the impression that at least the fundamental rights were thought of as higher law. The uncertainty about the status of fundamental rights contributed towards the confusion about the real relationship between directive principles and fundamental rights.

▼ The provisions originally included in the Bill of Rights to guarantee the right to property and to prescribe the way in which compensation for the expropriation of property should be paid were initially also formulated in an unsatisfactory way. The vagueness of these provisions led to a intense struggle between the judiciary and the legislature. In the process directive principles and fundamental rights were set up as direct opposites. Disputes about the expropriation of property were presented as a choice between following the directive principles or protecting fundamental rights. This attitude precluded a creative interrelationship between the fundamental rights and the directive principles. Only when the right to property lost its status as a fundamental right, did the courts began to truly use the fundamental rights and the directive principles in a creative way.

▼ The members of the constituent assembly also failed clearly to stipulate what role the directive principles should in fact play in the constitutional jurisprudence. They knew that most of the socio-economic rights could not be made directly enforceable by a court of law and shunted these rights into a separate section on directive principles. But when it had to decide what the role of these principles would be, it could only come up with the vague phrase that these

A Bill of Rights: Lessons from India

principles would be fundamental in the governance of the country. In the context of the strong positivist ideology associated with the British courts of the time—and therefore also with the Indian courts—this order could hardly have been expected to make sense to the judges, or have any immediate impact on their jurisprudence. Since it was stated emphatically in the constitution that the directive principles would be non-justiciable, the potential of these social and economic rights were not realised. Perhaps a more specific provision stating clearly the role of the directive principles in the judicial process, would have settled these principles as a formidable force from the outset.

6 SOCIO-ECONOMIC RIGHTS IN THE SOUTH AFRICAN CONSTITUTION

The South African Law Commission and the African National Congress both agree that socio-economic rights of some kind should be included in a Bill of Rights. Most parties also agree that the incorporation of social and economic rights are necessary to legitimise the whole constitution.[51] They differ however on how these rights should be formulated and enforced. I believe the Indian constitutional experience could be of great assistance in breaking this deadlock. If the drafters of the South African constitution are going to be serious about their commitment to the incorporation of socio-economic rights into the constitution, they would be well advised to look closely at the Indian experience. Quite a lot can be learnt from the mistakes made in the formulation of the relevant provisions. Even more revealing is the way in which the court reacted to these provisions and the ways in which it finally began to interpret them. Taking the Indian experience as my guideline, I would like to propose a specific approach to the incorporation of socio-economic rights in the South African constitution.

---

51. Didcott J.M., 'Practical workings of a Bill of Rights' in J. Van der Westhuizen and H.P. Viljoen (eds) *A Bill of Rights for South Africa* (1988) pp. 52-59.

6.1 Formulation of Socio-Economic Rights

I believe the basic premise of any Bill of Rights incorporated into a new South African constitution should be that both the traditional civil and political rights and the social and economic rights and principles should be included in it. It has been pointed out[52] that the distinction between 'negatively' enforceable civil and political rights, and social and economic rights which require positive action from the State, is a spurious one. Despite the fact that the socio-economic rights are sometimes less precise and therefore more difficult to enforce, *in principle*, they do not differ in any way from the civil and political rights. This principle should be reflected in a South African Bill of Rights.

The South African Law Commission and the De Klerk Government believed that only a limited group of socio-economic rights, formulated in the traditional negative way, should be included in a Bill of Rights. The commission is of the opinion that socio-economic rights formulated as positive orders or directive principles would be unenforceable and will therefore be of no practical value. It is my opinion that the Indian experience contradicts this view and I would argue that this approach should be rejected by anybody who is serious about drafting a Bill of Rights for South Africa with real relevance to the majority of the population.

The ANC's draft Bill of Rights does not draw any distinction between rights directly enforceable by a court of law and other rights and principles not directly enforceable by a court of law. The point of departure for the ANC is that there is no principled or philosophical difference between traditional first generation rights and socio-economic rights. This approach has merit, since it will ensure that the socio-economic rights and principles, which are more difficult to enforce, will not from the start be relegated to second-class status. Unfortunately the ANC's document is not always clear about which rights are to be directly enforceable by the courts and which rights are to be enforced only as directives to the State or in some other non-legal

---

52. E. Mureinik 'Beyond a charter of luxuries: economic rights in the constitution' *South African Journal of Human Rights* vol. 8 part 4 (1992) pp. 464-467; and N. Haysom 'Constitutionalism, majoritarian democracy and socio-economic rights' *South African Journal of Human Rights* vol. 8 part 4 (1992) pp. 451-457.

A Bill of Rights: Lessons from India

way. There is a real danger that this state of affairs will lead to confusion among the members of the judiciary concerning the role of those parts of the Bill of Rights not directly enforceable by them. This confusion could easily translate into inertia on the part of the judiciary, and many of the ringing principles set out in the ANC's Bill could then become mere adornments and pious wishes. This is in effect what happened in India where uncertainty about the application of fairly vague principles and other socio-economic rights led the Supreme Court through a series of destructive contortions, and paralysed the court for more than thirty years before it was finally able to unlock the potential of the directive principles.

To overcome this problem, I propose that the Bill of Rights included in a new South African constitution should contain not only traditional civil and political rights, but also social and economic rights and principles. At the same time this Bill should make a clear distinction between directly enforceable rights on the one hand, and those rights and principles not directly enforceable by the courts on the other. This could be done by including these different provisions in two separate Chapters of the Bill of Rights—one Chapter for directly enforceable rights, and another for other rights and principles.

It will be imperative to state clearly in such a Bill what the field of application of each section is. It will also have to be clearly stated in the Bill of Rights that the distinction between directly enforceable rights and non-enforceable rights and principles does not in any way rely on a principle that there is a conceptual difference—or any difference in status—between the rights enshrined in either Chapter of the Bill of Rights. In accordance with the ANC's approach, civil and political rights, for example, must not have any higher status than social and economic rights. All rights in both Chapters of the Bill of Rights must clearly be shown to have equal status, in so far as any two rights can ever have equal status. These rights will only differ in as far as they will be enforced through different mechanisms.

Such an approach will facilitate the incorporation of a wide variety of socio-economic rights and principles—as well as other important constitutional norms—into a Bill of Rights while potential problems with the enforcement and application of these rights will be effectively addressed.

In this regard, the writers of the South African constitution should look at the Indian constitutional jurisprudence to guide them when they decide on the possibilities for the application of the non-enforceable provisions.

6.2 Positive Enforceable Socio-Economic Rights

It took the Indian courts almost 40 years to realise that it was possible—in certain restricted situations—to place a positive duty on the State in order to ensure the realisation of a socio-economic right. This happened when the court started to utilise directive principles to 'discover' new rights in the recognised and enforceable rights—such as the right to equality and the right to life—and this enabled the courts to place a positive duty on the State to act in a certain manner or to attain certain goals. But the context-specific way in which these rights were discovered and enforced, resulted in a less than universal application of these new rights.

I believe it would be a mistake not to include certain socio-economic rights as directly and positively enforceable rights in the South African constitution. If the basic premise is that the only distinction between different rights in the two Chapters of the Bill of Rights is that some can be more easily enforced by the courts, it must follow that all rights which can apparently be directly enforced by the courts—whether civil and political or social and economic—should be included in the Chapter of directly enforceable rights. As Nicolas Haysom has pointed out, the distinction made between so-called first generation rights and second generation rights does not rest on subject matter, but on remedy. Accordingly, there can be no argument against the incorporation of socio-economic rights as directly enforceable rights in a Bill of Rights *per se*, only against rights which provide for no legal remedy for those denied the right concerned. As long as socio-economic rights are framed in a way which allows for their enforcement they can be accepted into the 'holy family'.[53] This is also in accordance with the Indian experience, which has shown that courts—in certain circumstances—have the capacity to enforce positive orders against the State or other institutions.

---

53. Haysom, N., 'Constitutionalism, majoritarian democracy and socio-economic rights' *South African Journal of Human Rights* vol 8 part 4 (1992) 458.

A Bill of Rights: Lessons from India

The incorporation of some socio-economic rights as positive enforceable rights in a Bill of Rights would represent a compromise between the ANC's draft Bill of Rights and that proposed by the South African Law Commission. Such an approach would endorse the ANC's view in as far as it relies on the assumption that there is no conceptual difference between civil and political rights on the one hand, and the social and economic rights on the other. But it is also in line with the strong view held by the Law Commission (and by the National Party) that a clear distinction should be made between enforceable rights and unenforceable rights and principles. This approach could, however, only be followed if the ANC discards its insistence that all rights and principles should be incorporated in a single, undivided, Bill of Rights, and if the National Party and the South African Law Commission discard their insistence that only negative enforceable rights could be included in a Bill of Rights.

Not all socio-economic rights would qualify for inclusion as positively enforceable rights. Only those rights which can be formulated with precision should be considered for possible inclusion in this category. A right would only be included as enforceable if its scope and limits can be described with a specific amount of certainty. It must also not be phrased in such a way that the court would be required in its enforcement of the rights to make policy decisions about the *way* in which these rights should be realised. As an unelected technical body, a court is specifically unsuited to make policy decisions about the realisation of rights. Only where such a right can be phrased in such a way that the courts could clearly enforce them without having to decide on how these rights should be realised, will they be candidates for inclusion. Finally, and most importantly, the realisation of these rights must be attainable from a financial point of view before they can be included as directly enforceable positive rights. Only those rights which it is agreed on beforehand would be affordable and within reach of the national budget, could be incorporated.

Possible candidates for inclusion could be: a right to legal representation; a right to free and compulsory education up to a certain level or up to a certain age; a right to running water; a right to primary health care; a right against starvation; and a right to access to electricity.

6.3 Non-enforceable Rights and Directive Principles

Many of the socio-economic rights and principles could, of course, not be included as directly enforceable rights in the first Chapter of the Bill of Rights. As rights with equal status to those rights included in the first Chapter, they will, however, have to be included in the second Chapter of the Bill of Rights. These rights and principles could be formulated as orders or directive principles to the State to achieve certain goals or keep certain principles in mind in the implementation of State policy. These provisions should be specifically phrased as unenforceable rights and principles to remove any possible confusion about their role.

Despite the fact that these rights and principles will not be made directly enforceable in a positive way by the courts, the Indian experience has taught us that the incorporation of these rights and principles as non-enforceable provisions would not preclude them from having a huge influence on constitutional jurisprudence. The scope of the influence of these non-enforceable rights and principles on the constitutional jurisprudence will depend on the nature of these provisions and the way in which the possibilities for application are set out in the constitution. The Indian experience shows us that the constitution must clearly state what the goal of the included non-enforceable right and directive is and what the relationship between these non-enforceable provisions and the enforceable provisions are. In order to ensure that the non-enforceable rights and principles have maximum influence, specific attention should be given to the following aspects.

6.4 Equal Status of all Rights in the Constitution

One of the major flaws in the Indian constitution was the failure of the constituent assembly—in its attempt to compromise and achieve consensus among its factions—clearly to stipulate what the relationship between the enforceable fundamental rights and the unenforceable directive principles was. These parts were set up as opposites and soon the court had to decide whether the fundamental rights could be restricted or infringed by legislation or executive actions which

A Bill of Rights: Lessons from India

represented an attempt to achieve the goals set out in the directive principles. This forced the court to see the fundamental rights and directive principles as in opposition to each other.

To counter this problem a South African constitution will have to state unequivocally that there is no difference in the *status* of the enforceable rights, on the one hand, and the non-enforceable rights and principles on the other. In this view the provisions in the unenforceable Chapter of the constitution—which would resemble Part IV on directive principles in the Indian constitution—will have to be seen as rights and principles which are guaranteed but which can not be directly enforced in a positive way by the courts. They are therefore taken up in a separate Chapter of the Bill of Rights to be enforced through other means. Such an approach would force the court to deal with *all* the rights on an equal basis, because they will be deemed to be the same in every single way except in the way in which they can be enforced. When these rights clash directly, the courts will have to decide on the matter in the same way any court practising judicial review decides cases where a clash between different principles in the Bill of Rights occur.

Such an approach constitutes a compromise between the approach taken by the South African Law Commission and the National Party Government on the one hand, and the ANC on the other. This approach would recognise the idea put forward by the ANC that there is no conceptual difference between civil and political rights and social and economic rights, while also giving a nod towards the Law Commission's idea that some socio-economic rights are not suitable for direct enforcement by the judiciary.

6.5 Role of Unenforceable Rights and Directive Principles in the Interpretation of Legislation

Including non-enforceable rights and principles and giving it equal status with enforceable rights will not, on its own, ensure its relevance and effectiveness. The Bill of Rights will also have to stipulate in what other ways these rights and principles could be enforced. A general and vague provision—such as the one included in the Indian constitution, which stated that the directive principles were fundamental in the governance of the country—will be inadequate. If the Bill of Rights is going to be a document of social transformation, stronger medicine will have to be prescribed.

As a first step, a new South African constitution will have to stipulate clearly that the non-enforceable provisions in the Bill of Rights will operate as guidelines to the court in any decision they make. The relevant provision will have to make it clear that the Bill of Rights should be read and interpreted as a holistic document and that both the enforceable and the non-enforceable provisions should be taken into account in the interpretation of both *legislation and the common law*. The provision could direct the courts to take into account *all the provisions of the Bill of Rights* in its interpretation of legislation—also private law legislation. The court could also be directed to take into account all the provisions of the Bill of Rights where it has to determine the validity of subordinate legislation or administrative acts.

This approach would be in accordance with the views of both the ANC and the South African Law Commission. Both these groups agree that all the provisions of the Bill of Rights should be used in the interpretation of legislation.

6.6 Negative Enforcement of Unenforceable Rights and Directive Principles

So far, I have tried to distinguish between the two Chapters of the Bill of Rights, on the grounds that the rights in one Chapter would be directly enforceable. Where social and economic rights are included in this Chapter, the court would have the power to make an order which places a positive duty on the State to ensure the realisation of these rights. But where it appears impossible—by the nature of the socio-economic right—to include it as a directly enforceable right in the Bill of Rights, it does not suggest that the courts would not be able to enforce these rights in a purely negative way.

It took the Indian Supreme Court more than 30 years before it came to the point where it could invalidate the actions of the State or other institutions which infringed upon the socio-economic rights set out in the directive principles. The power to do this was never explicitly

A Bill of Rights: Lessons from India

conferred on the court. Only after the Indian courts started using the directive principles to read into the right to life also the right to livelihood and the right to a healthy environment, did they start to prohibit actions which threatened these rights.

I believe a new South African constitution should contain a provision to authorise the courts to prohibit a relevant institution to act in such a way as to constitute a substantial infringement on the utilisation or realisation of one of the non-enforceable socio-economic rights. This would ensure at least some kind of enforcement of the rights and principles set out in the non-enforceable Chapter of the Bill of Rights. Where the intended action by the State or other institution threatens an immediate and serious infringement or interference of one of the rights or principles set out in the Chapter dealing with directive principles, the court could be authorised to protect these rights and principles by giving the appropriate order to prohibit the intended action. Where a non-enforceable provision places a burden on the State to take steps to guarantee the right to housing of all citizens, the court could, for example, prohibit the State from bulldozing the squatter shacks on State land unless alternative housing is also provided for.

Depending on the formulation of the empowering clause, the courts could obtain far-reaching powers. This would not necessarily entangle the courts in policy decisions—in deciding, for example, how the State should go about guaranteeing the right to housing to all citizens. No right—be it directly enforceable by the courts or not—is absolute. As is the case with enforceable rights, the court would have to decide in every case whether the planned infringement on the right or principle is reasonable and just, given the constitutional commitment to democracy, freedom, and social and economic equality. As Mureinik has pointed out, in exercising its function of judicial review a court usually asks: given the constitutional commitment to one of the rights guaranteed in the Bill of Rights, can the action or planned action complained of be justified.[54] The court will then have the power to declare parliamentary legislation invalid if it infringes in an unreasonable way on the protection of the non-enforceable rights, or where it hampers the realisation of these rights.

---

54. Mureinik 'Beyond a charter of luxuries: economic rights in the constitution' *South African Journal of Human Rights* vol. 8 part 4 (1992) 472.

This approach is in accordance with Article 19(12) of the ANC's draft Bill of Rights. This Article declares:

> Where justice and the achievement of the objectives of the Bill of Rights so require, the State or any private body or individual may be restrained by the Courts from doing anything which interferes with or reduce enjoyment of these rights or impedes their realisation.

This approach also seems to be consistent with the South African Law Commission's view that the duty of the court should be to declare void all State action which infringes on the rights protected in the Bill of Rights.

6.7 Judicial Review of Legislation

Finally, the courts could perhaps be given the far-reaching power to invalidate *legislation* which has clearly contributed to the economic deprivation or has been, or still is, a major obstacle in the realisation of non-enforceable rights and directive principles. Some political groups might believe this to be too far-reaching a proposal. I would not agree with such a view because this power will, in a way, be a logical consequence of the basic principle underlying the Bill of Rights that directly enforceable rights and non-enforceable rights will have the same status. Just as the court will have the power to determine whether any law contravenes one of the enforceable rights, it should have the power to determine whether any of these laws contravenes one of the unenforceable rights and principles. The court will, of course, not have the power to order the State to act positively to ensure these rights for the applicants, but the court will have the power to identify those laws which partly caused or contributed to the infringement of any of the socio-economic rights. To contend with expected criticism, the power of the court could be restricted to scrutinise only legislation which was adopted in the era before the democratically elected government came to power. This will ensure that the judges of the court (which might turn out to be rather conservative) do not interfere with the social legislation of the democratically elected Parliament.

The innovative—but context specific—application of directive principles by the Indian Supreme Court did not reach as far as scrutinising legislation which might have caused some of the socio-economic deprivation among the population. Where injustice and social and economic deprivation resulted directly from pre-independence legislation, the Indian courts refrained from declaring such legislation invalid.[55] I believe this was a mistake.

Learning from the Indian experience, a South African constitution could perhaps contain a provision empowering the court to declare invalid any of the pre-democratic legislation which had clearly contributed to the socio-economic deprivation of the majority of the population or had clearly been a major obstacle in the realisation of the non-enforceable rights and principles. The court could then exercise its power in cases where applicants contend that they are being deprived of the realisation of one or other non-enforceable socio-economic rights. As part of its function of judicial review, the court will then have the power to consider whether the offending law infringes upon one of the rights guaranteed in the Bill of Rights. If it does, the court will have the power to declare the law invalid.

As is the case in all other circumstances of judicial review, the court will scrutinise the legislation to find out if, given the constitutional commitment to social and economic rights, the legislation constitutes an unreasonable infringement on those rights. If the court finds that the legislation is reasonably necessary to achieve a legitimate State interest, it will not be invalidated. However, if the court finds that it contributed, or still contributes greatly, to the poverty and deprivation among the population and it does not serve any legitimate State interest, it could be invalidated.

Neither the ANC's draft Bill nor the South African Law Commission includes any similar provisions in their draft Bills, but I believe this concept does not directly contradict the approach of either party. It coincides with the Law Commission's idea that judicial review should be a matter of measuring legislation against the Bill of Rights, while the ANC would clearly welcome suggestions for the effective enforcement of these rights.

---

55. Singh *JILI* 254.

7 CONCLUSION

The fundamental realisation that, in principle, there is no real difference between the so-called first generation rights and the so-called second generation rights, opens up a variety of possibilities for the incorporation and enforcement of such rights. In this paper I have tried to come up with a scheme through which all the important rights can be incorporated *and*—in some way or the other—enforced.

I have tried to come up with a few suggestions about the alternative forms of enforcement for different rights. The Indian experience has shown that the potential for any such mechanism should not be underestimated.

It would be dangerous, however, merely to include all social and economic rights as a 'shopping list' in a Bill of Rights with the vague hope that the judiciary would stir the pot to come up with innovative enforcement mechanisms. It is the duty of the constitutional writers—not of the courts—to stipulate clearly what these mechanisms are. Failure to do so could turn the Bill of Rights into a charter for the rich and powerful, a discredited document without anything to say to the poor and destitute population of South Africa.

Chapter Five

The Protection of Property in South Africa

Andrew Caiger

> *For it is the dawn that has come, as it has come for a thousand centuries, never failing. But when that dawn will come, of our emancipation, from fear of bondage and the bondage of fear, why, that is a secret.*[1]

1 INTRODUCTION

South Africans are currently negotiating their future. The process has been a long, arduous, and particularly violent one. The constitutional dispensation resulting from these negotiations is likely to be radically different from the present one—it would formally spell the end to the apartheid era which has been part of the South African heritage longer than most people realise.[2] The new constitutional dispensation is likely to include a justiciable Bill of Rights and it is the content of this which is most hotly contested. In particular there has been a very healthy debate concerning the protection of property in a new post-apartheid South Africa.

The African National Congress was not initially in favour of such a Bill of Rights. There was a justified suspicion that the purpose of a Bill

---

1. Alan Paton, *Cry the Beloved Country* (Penguin).
2. Ordinance 49/1828 (Cape) required black people to carry passes in order to enter the Cape Colony and a pass was also required before they could seek employment.

of Rights so keenly promoted by liberal legal scholars—and of late even by some conservatives—was to entrench and protect white privilege. The ANC felt that its Freedom Charter[3] was sufficient protection for all in a democratic South Africa. In 1991 the ANC adopted its own proposals for a Bill of Rights which is substantially based on the spirit of the Freedom Charter.[4]

The vital issue of interest to all South Africans is, what is the future policy with regard to property likely to be in a country where the white sector of the population, constituting 14 per cent of the population, own about 87 per cent of the land.[5]

Since the 1991 abolition of the Land Acts (of 1913 and 1936) and their replacement by new land statutes,[6] white property owners have become fearful of losing their property. This is especially the case with white farmers, many of whom are likely to face disputes over land ownership, especially in the face of ANC promises of redress of past wrongs in this regard. Many Transvaal farmers marched to Pretoria after the publication of the White Paper on Land Reform in November 1990 and demanded to meet with the State President in order to seek

---

3. The Freedom Charter of the ANC was adopted at the Congress of the People at Kliptown, Johannesburg, on June 25 and 26, 1955. See also Albert Luthuli, *Let My People Go* (Fontana, 1963). The Charter was considered very progressive, even radical, by some in the 1950s and there is still a strong attachment to the principles of the Freedom Charter. The section concerned with property will be dealt with below.

4. 'A Bill of Rights for a Democratic South Africa—Working Draft for consultation', *South African Journal of Human Rights* (1991), p. 110. For comments on the ANC proposals see: Haysom, N. 'Democracy, Constitutionalism and the ANC's Bill of Rights for a new South Africa', *South African Journal of Human Rights* (1991), p. 102; Marcus, G and Davis, D. D. Judicial Review under an ANC Government', *South African Journal of Human Rights* (1991) p. 93; van Wyk, D. 'Die ANC se Konsephandves van Menseregte—'n paar opmerkings', *Tydskrif van Hedendaagse Romeins-Hollands Reg* (1991) p. 105.

5. Dugard, J. 'Towards Genuine Democracy in Conflict-Ridden Countries: A South African Perspective', Beyond Law: *Mas Alla Del Derecho*, 1 (1991), p. 56.

6. The statutes abolishing and replacing the Land Acts of 1913 (the Black Land Act 27 of 1913) and 1936 (the Development Trust and Land Act 18 of 1936) are the Abolition of Racially Based Land Measures Act 108 of 1991; the Upgrading of Land Tenure Rights Act 112 of 1991 and the Less Formal Township Establishment Act 113 of 1991.

clarity on this point. The Government's White Paper on Land Reform[7] reasserted the status quo as far as land ownership was concerned. As regards the access to land by blacks, provision was made for such access through the establishment of 'less formal' townships, thus providing for formally approved squatting, with other access to land left to the market to sort out.

The Land Acts formed the basis of land allocation between black and white in South Africa, providing the basis on which blacks could be excluded not only from access to land, but also from its control. The fear among urban white property owners is that the value of their properties is likely to drop once the Government's new 'policies' come into operation.[8]

The De Klerk Government was faced with dispossessed people occupying land they previously lived on, and other landless people moving onto any land where they could make a home, on which they could farm, or where they could live within easy access to their work. The Government's response to these challenges was piecemeal, accommodating some claims and resisting others. On the one hand the Government allocated substantial resources (R600 million) for the purchase and development of serviced sites—official squatting. In other cases, such as the Hout Bay squatters, the Government tried to accommodate them through the purchase of land in Hout Bay, while in the case of Goedgevonden (in the western Transvaal) the Government resisted squatter claims.[9]

The conundrum facing a new government is how to bring about an equitable redistribution of land with as little injustice as possible. This problem about property becomes more acute when it becomes a question of including property protection in a Bill of Rights. A Bill of Rights which does not guarantee the protection of property will hardly be worth its salt and will fall foul of any liberal notions of protection of rights. However, Ng'ong'ola has shown that the legal protection of property, especially land, in a Bill of Rights is problematic.[10] Thus the

---

7. WP B-91.
8. Hansard (South African Parliamentary Debates), 20th March 1991, col 3339-3342; 16th April 1991, col 1035-1040.
9. Hansard, 16th April 1991, col 1041-1042; 14th May 1991, col 8501-8512; 26th February 1991, col 215-221.
10. Ng'ong'ola, C. 'The Post-Colonial era in relation to land expropriation laws in Botswana, Malawi, Zambia and Zimbabwe', *International and Comparative Law Quarterly Review* (1992) p. 117.

first problem which has to be addressed is how two seemingly contradictory policies can be reconciled: the protection of property and redistribution of property within a Bill of Rights framework. The ANC has been advised that it would be best to approach a constitutional future in South Africa with a justiciable Bill of Rights—thus providing a legal basis within which state policy may be pursued. Another reason why the ANC might have been persuaded to accept a 'Rights' paradigm is the fact that South Africa will probably be seeking international aid and will want to encourage foreign investment. A familiar liberal legal paradigm might serve a useful ideological purpose in promoting economic regeneration of the economy.[11]

The second and related issue is whether a future government is likely to pursue a policy of land ownership for all South Africans, or whether it will be more concerned with ensuring access to land. It is likely that a new government will adopt a pragmatic, if contradictory, approach to this problem. The reason for this may be found in the historical roots of the country, most notably those which affect the distribution of land. Should the former avenue be pursued, it is doubtful whether the Government will have adequate resources to expropriate land on a scale sufficient to satisfy even some of the demand.

Guaranteeing access to the land seems to be a more pragmatic approach for several reasons. Most 'white' land ownership is in terms of the common law—that means that the owner has dominium over the land he lives on, although the law has been accommodated to make provision for ownership of sectional titles (in the case of apartments or town houses) and time and space-sharing of holiday accommodation. Most blacks in South Africa have held land in terms of the Black Administration Act cf 1927 which regulated access to land in the urban

---

11. See for example Yash Ghai, 'The Role of Law in the Transition of Societies: The African Experience', *Journal of African Law*, (1991), p.8. At p.20 Ghai notes: 'This intervention (by the State in transforming the apartheid social and market processes) need not be mediated through law, but there may be a number of good reasons to do so. South Africa's position in the international economy cannot be changed overnight, and the dominant role to transitional capital would suggest that change in relations may be easier to manage through law. An emphasis on law may also be necessary to maintain the democratic nature of the state and to canvas and mobilise public support for change'.

areas, and the hated Land Acts of 1913 and 1936 which partitioned South Africa into white areas and black areas where the use of the land was either determined by customary law or statute. In the case of the latter, statutory innovations such as quitrent and permission to occupy land applied.

It has always been difficult to describe the nature of these 'rights' in terms of traditional common law concepts. At best they have been seen as 'rights' not to be proceeded against. But in addition to the statutory framework[12] a few blacks had freehold and others had informal arrangements with white farmers. Sol Plaatje, writing after the passing of the Land Act of 1913, notes that about one million black South Africans (20 per cent) out of four and a half million were squatters. He explains:

> A squatter in South Africa is a native who owns some livestock and, having no land of his own hires a farm or grazing and ploughing rights from a land owner, to raise grain for his own use and feed his stock. Hence, these squatters are hit very hard.[13]

These tenancies or squatter rights could be registered, but some were merely verbal contracts for which no registration was required. The effect of the 1913 Land Act was to force many blacks off the land or subject them to wage labour either on the farms or in the mines.[14] Yet many of them remained on these farms under verbal contracts for which no registration was required and no protection offered.

Thus precedent exists for shared access to land and this is now a real possibility as the discriminatory aspects of the Land Acts have been repealed.

---

12. For details of the statutory framework governing the access/occupation of land by black people see: Van der Walt A.J., 'Land Law without the Land Acts—predicaments and possibilities', *Tydskrif van Hedendaagse Romeins-Hollands Reg* (1991), p. 738; Robertson, C. 'Black land tenure: disabilities and some rights', in Rycroft, A. (ed.), *Race and the Law in South Africa*, (Juta & Co., 1987, Cape Town); Sachs, A. *Justice in South Africa* (Chatto, Heinemann, 1973, London).
13. Plaatje, Sol *Native Life in South Africa* (Ravan Press, Johannesburg), pp. 21-22.
14. Wickens, P.L. 'The Natives Land Act of 1913: A cautionary essay on simple explanations of complex change', *South African Journal of Economics* (1981) p. 105.

2 RECENT DEVELOPMENTS

2.1 The Importance of Land in South Africa

The land exercises a special force in the psyche of South Africans. No one who has ever lived in Africa for a period of time can be left untouched by the breathtaking majesty of its scenery. South Africa is especially beautiful having several different climates in one country coupled with a dramatic topography. The land forms part of every African's rite of passage. When young men are circumcised their blood drips onto the land in a symbolic link to it. Afrikaners also have shed blood for the land they live on and so their connection to it is no less strong, though perhaps it is different. Other South Africans share a love for their land simply because they have been able to live there.

One of the problems concerning land in South Africa is the different perceptions of its value in as far as property is concerned. Most whites see the land as something that can be owned—a right which can be asserted against the world at large and be used to the exclusion of others.

The traditions of the land for Africans are quite different. Traditionally they do not see the land as being capable of being owned but rather used. Statutory treatment of African land has only served to reinforce these values, albeit in a distorted manner. Only in the Cape could black people actually own land in accordance with the common law and this capability was abolished in 1936 when the black franchise was effectively abrogated.

African land therefore traditionally formed part of the social obligations within the community and could not be transferred through succession. Bennett notes that, quoting Holleman:

> ...land, whether cultivated or uncultivated, was never regarded as 'wealth' or even 'property' in the ordinary sense, and therefore did not form part of a person's estate... Land is not property (*cinhu»*), it is something you use for a time and then abandon.[15]

It seems that in southern Africa rights of access to land could be

---

15. Bennett, T.W. *Sourcebook of African Customary Law*, (Juta & Co., 1991, Cape Town), p. 388.

inheritable depending on population density, land shortages and soil impoverishment.[16]

2.2 Previous Government Policy and Jurisprudence with Regard to Property

The De Klerk Government's land policy had several dimensions and is best described in Afrikaans as *ontoereikend*—insufficient or inadequate or deficient. On the one hand there was a recognition that land must be made available on which 'squatters' or displaced people can live since the Government no longer has the power to uproot people and compel them to live where directed. Government action in this regard has been pre-empted by squatters settling on land as they pleased. Responding to this crisis the Government passed the Less Formal Township Establishment Act[17] giving the Administrator of each of the four provinces extensive powers to establish these less formal townships within various metropolitan areas of South Africa. These townships aimed at providing the newly arrived 'squatter' or inhabitant with a surveyed plot on which he/she could squat in an 'orderly' fashion. In addition the most rudimentary services such as water provision, dusty roads, refuse removal and aquaprivy toilets (a type of biological toilet with septic tank) were provided. No electricity was guaranteed. These less formal townships were invariably situated close to suburbs populated predominantly by whites. The latter had complained of an increased crime rate, devalued properties and increased pollution and there was considerable resistance to this government policy—residents basically adopting the 'not in my back yard' approach. Recently the powers of the Administrator of the Transvaal were successfully challenged in court. A community of interest, no doubt spawned by an apartheid legacy, was established by the Diepsloot Residents and Landowners. They applied for and were granted an interim interdict (interlocutory injunction) against the Administrator of the Transvaal arguing that the proposed 'Less Formal' township in their area was likely to constitute a public nuisance in that there would be increased pollution in the form of dust, smoke and contaminated water from the

---

16. Bennett, above, n. 15, p. 389.
17. Act 113 of 1991.

sanitation. They also successfully argued that there was likely to be an increased crime rate as was the case in Midrand (between Johannesburg and Pretoria) where the crime rate had reached unbearable proportions.[18] This case provides a typical example of the type of action which whites are taking to protect their rights of ownership. The following comments of the court are instructive regarding the use of the common law to protect property rights:

> Great play has been made of the words 'less formal settlement' and 'less formal manner'. These words, in particular, have been relied upon for the argument that the Legislature intended to justify an interference with the common law rights of third parties.
>
> In my view, there are no indications in the Act that the Legislature intended to justify an interference with the common law rights of third persons where such an interference amounts to a public nuisance.[19]

While adopting this ad hoc policy of less formal townships, the Government has found itself in the difficult position of having to defend the property rights of irate farmers on *inter alia* the farm of Goedgevonden. This case involved the return of a dispossessed black community which once collectively owned and lived on this farm but which was told to leave at the end of 1978 when it was sent to land in Bophutatswana, one of the independent Homelands. The removal of these people left them much worse off on their new farms. Having less land available to them, they could not sustain a sufficient level of agricultural production to provide a viable living.

After they left, that farm and other neighbouring farms were let to white farmers. Technically the farms belonged to the Government and constituted part of its Trust land, so it was perfectly entitled to return this land to the black community it had dispossessed several years earlier. This case attracted considerable international attention when the lessee farmers teamed up with the Afrikaner Resistance Movement (AWB) in order to remove this community forcibly from the

---

18. *Diepsloot Residents & Landowners* v. *Administrator, Transvaal* 1993 (1) SALR 577.
19. Above, n. 18, p. 584 B-C.

Goedgevonden farm.[20] This case makes sad reading and although the judge was sympathetic, the Government (in the name of the afflicted farmers) was granted a spoliation order evicting these dispossessed people.[21]

Different approaches were adopted by the Government in the cases of the Port Nolloth and Hout Bay squatters. In the former the squatters were settled on municipal land around Port Nolloth (which is close to the Namibian border) belonging to the Port Nolloth Municipality. They were settled there after they were evicted from a farm in Namibia. Many of the squatters had family members working in Port Nolloth and on the alluvial diamond mines at the mouth of the Orange river (the South African/Namibian border). The Government and the Port Nolloth Municipality reached an agreement that the squatters were to be provided with land on which to erect the shelters and tents they were to be given. Many of these squatters erected more permanent structures.

In the case of Hout Bay the Government actually found land on which these squatters could be settled.[22] There had been considerable squatting on private land in the Hout Bay area and owners of such property obtained eviction orders from the courts after the police failed to take any action against the squatters. The police said they did not enforce the anti-squatting law for fear of adverse publicity.[23] Many of these squatters were gainfully employed in Hout Bay.

In both the Port Nolloth and Hout Bay cases legal action was brought challenging squatter land occupation. These actions have usually been brought either as a request for an injunction in terms of the common law spoliation remedy (Mandament van Spolie), or as statutory remedies against squatting provided for in the Prevention of Illegal Squatting Act (The Squatting Act).[24]

The essence of a spoliation action is that the person who asks for the spoliation order must establish possession—this need not be lawful possession, but the possession must be for the benefit of the possessor and not for someone else. In addition the person must establish that he

---

20. Hansard, 14th May 1991, col 8449-8512.
21. *Minister of Agriculture and Agricultural Development and Others* v. *Segopolo and Others* 1992 (3) SALR 944, at 974 *et seq.*
22. Hansard, 26th February 1991, col 215-221.
23. *Beyers and others* v. *Mlanjeni and others* 1991 (2) SALR 392 (C).
24. Act 52 of 1951.

is unlawfully deprived of possession. The purpose of the action is to establish the *status quo ante* so that the merits of the respective claims can be considered at a later stage. Perhaps the most important rationale for the action is the principle of Roman-Dutch law that no persons should take the law into their own hands.[25]

The purpose of the Squatting Act is also to protect property rights of either the lessee or owner. Several remedies are available under the legislation. A complaint can be made to the police and the squatters can be prosecuted for trespass, and on conviction an eviction order may be made. The owner may choose to approach his local authority and ask it to demolish the squatter's dwelling. The local authority may proceed with demolition without a court order. The squatter may respond by applying for a spoliation order. The chances of the squatter successfully defending his land occupation would seem to depend on the person or body against whom the defence is raised. Should the defence be raised against a local authority such as a municipality, and there are many squatters who might be affected by the outcome of the decision, then it is probable that the spoliation defence will be successful. Where the spoliation is raised by a squatter as a defence against a private landowner or lessee then the defence is less likely to succeed.[26]

Where local authorities are involved, the courts have held on two separate occasions that there is an obligation on the local authority to consider what is to become of the squatters. The courts are concerned that the problem of itinerant squatters is not passed from one local authority to another and therefore a duty is placed on a local authority to attempt to find a remedy for the squatting predicament. In these cases the squatters have usually gained permission for a temporary sojourn and once permission has been given it becomes more difficult to remove them.[27] In the *Port Nolloth* case[28] the predominantly white

---

25. *Yeko* v. *Qana*, 1973 (4) SALR 735 (A); Taitz, J. (1982) SALJ, p. 36; de Waal M.J. 'Die Mandament van Spolie—Meer as besitherstel?' (1977) *Responsa Meridiana*.
26. *Kgosana and Another* v. *Otto*, 1991 (2) SALR 113 W; *Beyers and others* v. *Mlanjeni and others* 1991 (2) SALR 392 (C).
27. *Kayamandi Town Council* v. *Mkhwaso and others* 1991 (2) SALR 630 (W); *Port Nolloth Municipality* v. *Xhalisa and others; Luwalala and others* v. *Port Nolloth Municipality* 1991 (3) SALR 98.
28. *Ibid.* Also see Caiger, A. `The judicial function in `post' apartheid South Africa: Some recent cases and trends', Law & Society Meeting working paper, Philadelphia, May 1992.

residents had brought pressure to bear on the municipality to have the 'squatters' removed. They had initially been settled there after the Government had intervened and given certain undertakings regarding their stay. When the municipality sought to enforce the Squatting Act a spoliation order was successfully brought to counter the local authority's action. In a remarkable judgment which bristles with formalistic ingenuity it was held that the Squatting Act did not apply to lawful occupation—inferring that the local authority could not withdraw permission once given; and finally, that only structures could be demolished in terms of the Act. A tent was not a structure and could only be struck or taken down.[29]

From the above examples it is clear that the courts were willing to extend the protection of the common law to ordinary individuals on a fairly generous basis while placing obstacles in the way of government action vis à vis individuals or groups of individuals. There was a clear recognition that government is in a better position to deal with squatter problems than the individual.

Government initiative with regard to making adequate land available for the occupation of squatters or landless people—for much of which it must bear direct responsibility—was fragmentary and incoherent. It would seem that the Government and squatters were likely to have more success in providing access to land where this happened on a piecemeal and/or a negotiated manner. Where a more formalistic route had been pursued, such as in the case of the Less Formal Township Establishment Act, the successful opposition of the Diepsloot community prevented the establishment of a 'formal' squatter camp.

Moreover, it is clear that the Government had no coherent intention of implementing policies of land redress—which they could do with respect to Trust land which they owned. It is estimated that the Government still had not completed the purchases required to satisfy the 1936 Land Act quotas[30] although it was decided to release more Trust land for Black occupation. Most of this land was adjacent to the Homelands and seemed destined to be incorporated in them.

---

29. *Port Nolloth Municipality* (fn 27, *supra*) at 115H.
30. Native Trust and Land Act of 1936 establishing the South African Development Trust in whom all Trust land vests. Also see Robertson, above, n. 12.

3 LAND REFORM? SOME PROPOSALS AND PROPOSITIONS

Assuming that a Bill of Rights is adopted in the new South African constitutional order, the question remains—how a future government can, or is likely to, respond to the conundrum of protecting property rights on the one hand and redistributing land on the other. In short, how will the past wrongs of apartheid be redressed with regard to land, bearing in mind that about 80 per cent or more of this land is owned by the white sector of the population?

This is a problem with which legal scholars have grappled since 1990. The first point to make is that none of the main negotiating parties at CODESA (or its successors) have provided a grand design. The ANC probably provides one of the most explicit approaches to the property issue—especially land. On close analysis its draft constitutional provisions provided ambiguous protection for property rights.

The Freedom Charter provides a good starting point for the ANC's original view. It declares:

> Restriction of land ownership on a racial basis shall be ended, and all the land redivided amongst those who work it, to banish famine and land hunger;

and

> All shall have the right to occupy land wherever they choose...[31]

The ANC Bill of Rights proposal dealt with Land and Property in Article 11. The following clauses are particularly relevant:

> 11.2 All men and women and lawfully constituted bodies are entitled to the peaceful enjoyment of their possession, including the right to acquire, own, or dispose of property in any part of the country without distinction based on race, colour, language, gender or creed.[32]

---

31. See Luthuli, above, n. 3, p. 213.
32. Above, n. 6. This right already exists in terms of the abolition of discriminatory provisions regarding land measures which include the relevant discriminatory provisions of the Group Areas Act 36 of 1966.

11.5 The State may by legislation take steps to overcome the effects of past statutory discrimination in relation to enjoyment of property rights.

11.7 No persons or legal entities shall be deprived of their possessions except on grounds of public interest or public utility, including the achievement of the objectives of the Constitution.

11.9 Compensation shall be just, taking into account the need to establish an equitable balance between public interest and the interest of those affected.

11.11 The preceding provisions shall not be interpreted as in any way impeding the right of the State to adopt such measures as might be deemed necessary in any democratic society for the control, use or acquisition of property in accordance with the general interest, or to preserve the environment...[33]

It is difficult to reconcile these provisions with the protection of property as part of first generation rights. Clearly where expropriation does occur the State will not be bound by market values, but compensation will be subject to an 'equitable balance' between individual interest and public interest. The latter is an interesting and necessary notion for a proper development of property law, especially with regard to land. Interestingly, nothing was said about how prompt the payment of compensation would be and whether it could be taken out of the country.

Clauses 11.5 to 11.11 echo similar provisions of South Africa's neighbours, more particularly Zambia and Zimbabwe, where the power of the State vis à vis the land owner has been strengthened. In

---

33. Bill of Rights for a democratic South Africa—Working draft for consultation', *South African Journal of Human Rights* (1991), p. 110; van Wyk, D. 'Die ANC se konsephandves van menseregte—'n paar opmerkings', *Tydskrif van Hedendaagse Romeins-Hollands Reg* (1991) p. 105; Haysom, N. 'Democracy, Constitutionalism and the ANC's Bill of Rights for a new South Africa', *South African Journal of Human Rights* (1991) p. 102.

particular the constitutional protection of what is called 'settler' land ownership has been weakened in these states since independence.

Ng'ong'ola[34] points out that in the decolonization process it was usual for the colonial power to protect 'settler' land ownership through constitutional means—usually in a Bill of Rights. Nigeria and Kenya were decolonized in the early 1960s. Both the Nigerian and Kenyan constitutions restrained the power of the State compulsorily to acquire land. Both provided for the lawful compulsory acquisition of 'settler' land with a right to adequate compensation for the land so acquired. The acquisition and compensation could be challenged in the High Court.[35] The Kenyan constitution most clearly reflected the standard terms of land acquisition. Four conditions had to be satisfied before land could be compulsorily acquired. Firstly, the taking must have been necessary

> in the interests of defence, public safety, public order, public morality, public health, town and country planning or the development or utilization of any property...to promote the public benefit.

Secondly, the necessity must have been—

> such as to afford reasonable justification for causing any hardship that may result.

The third condition provided for 'prompt payment' of 'full compensation'. At the same time, the expropriatee was entitled to repatriation of compensation, free of taxes and other deductions, to any country of his choice.[36]

It is clear that these provisions only provide relative protection of property since the derogations are of such a nature as considerably to weaken property rights. Yet it would be a mistake to assume that these protections were superficial. They would be effective, for example, where the State could not afford 'adequate compensation'.

In Central Africa land rights were weakened after independence. This was achieved by changing the basis of compulsory land acquisition

---

34. Ng'ong'ola, above, n. 10.
35. *Ibid.* p. 121 *et seq.*
36. *Ibid.* p. 122-123.

The Protection of Property in South Africa

and the basis of compensation. In general the law was amended to make State acquisition of land easier, by removing the need to pay adequate compensation for land acquired and by removing access to the courts. The constitutions of Zambia, Malawi, and Zimbabwe were accordingly amended to reflect the State's need to acquire land at less than 'adequate' compensation and the rights to land ownership were considerably weakened.[37] Malawi, for example, removed the Bill of Rights imposed on it and replaced it with a Statement of Fundamental Principles which did not really protect land ownership.[38] In addition Lands Acquisition Acts were passed by both Malawi and Zambia.[39]

Zambia's constitutional amendments removed the right to 'prompt payment' and repatriation and now allow the National Assembly to determine the principles of assessment and compensation for land which cannot be challenged in a court of law.[40]

Perhaps the issue of compensation illustrates the most significant shift in the weakening of the protection of land ownership. The Zambian Act provides the clearest example of this point providing that there would be no compensation for undeveloped or unutilized land, and only limited compensation where the absentee landlord had brought about 'unexhausted improvements' on unutilized land.[41] 'Unexhausted improvements' are defined in section 15(6) of the Act[42] as

> any quality permanently attached to the land directly resulting from expenditure of capital or labour and increasing the productive capacity, utility or amenity therefore, but does not include the results of ordinary cultivation other than standing crops or growing produce.

The definition of undeveloped or unutilized land depends on whether such land is located within an urban or rural area. The fact that the property is fenced or hedged does not imply that it is developed—that would depend on its locality.[43] No compensation which is payable may

---

37. *Ibid.* p. 124 *et seq.*
38. *Ibid.* p. 125.
39. *Ibid.* p. 127; Lands Acquisition Act No. 2 of 1970 (Zambia); Lands Acquisition Act No. 21 of 1970.
40. *Ibid.* p. 126.
41. *Ibid.* p. 129.
42. *Ibid.* p. 130.
43. *Ibid.*

exceed the market value. Payment of compensation is no longer prompt but is determined by ministerial discretion. Ng'ong'ola notes:[44]

> The main attraction of these changes in the principles for the assessment of compensation is that they appear to solve the problem of paying 'full', 'market value' compensation for undeveloped or underutilized land.

The Zimbabwean constitution provides an interesting recent example of the weakening of the protection of land ownership. The Zimbabwean constitution was the product of the Lancaster House settlement and therefore provided some protection for land ownership primarily of the white minority. The constitution authorised only the 'acquisition of 'under-utilized' land for the settlement of land for agricultural purposes.' The acquisition of land had to be reasonably necessary in the interests of specified 'public purposes' and there had to be 'prompt payment' and 'adequate' compensation.[45] These provisions were intended to protect the substantial white, especially farming, population, but they also served to frustrate government attempts at land redistribution. These provisions were to remain in place for ten years. In 1990 the Zimbabwe constitution was amended to remove the protection of property clause (clause 16). The effects of the constitutional amendments were described in a memorandum which accompanied the Constitution of Zimbabwe Amendment Bill (No 11 1990):

> The effect of the amendments will be as follows. Firstly, land, including utilised land, buildings and improvements to land, will be capable of being acquired for settlement, land reorganisation, environmental conservation, the utilization of natural resources or the relocation of persons... Secondly, the compensation payable for compulsory acquisition will have to be 'fair' and to be paid within a reasonable time: at present it must be 'adequate' and paid 'promptly'. Thirdly, Parliament would be allowed to specify principles on which the amount of compensation for the acquisition of land is to be assessed, to fix the amount of compensation in accordance with such principles, and to fix the period within which such

---

44. Ng'ong'ola, above, n. 10 p. 131.
45. Ng'ong'ola, above, n. 10 p. 132.

compensation will be paid. Fourthly, the absolute right granted by section 16(5) and (6) of the Constitution, to remit compensation out of the country, will be abolished. Fifthly, our courts will be allowed to order forfeiture of property for breaches of foreign law as well as breaches of Zimbabwean law; this will allow the proceeds of international crimes to be forfeited. And, finally, it will be made clear that section 16 of the Constitution does not apply to the extinction of debts gratuitously incurred by the Government.[46]

The amendments show, once again, a familiar pattern:

▼ Easier access of the state to land acquisition;

▼ Different and less favourable criteria for assessing compensation for land from 'adequate' to 'fair' compensation, although the latter may be just as problematic although provision is made for Parliament to define what it means by 'fair';

▼ Payment need no longer be 'prompt' but must be paid within 'a reasonable time'—a concept which is also problematic;

▼ Abolition of repatriation of compensation—this is hardly unreasonable in the case of Zimbabwe as it was also not allowed under the former regime;

▼ Finally, section 16(2) provides that the assessment of compensation cannot be challenged in a court of law.[47] The explanation proffered for removing the jurisdiction of the court to consider assessment of compensation is to avoid conflict between the judiciary and the executive arms of government. A second, less important, reason may be the fact that the court may have difficulty in agreeing what constitutes 'adequate' or 'fair' compensation.

Experience seems to indicate that the law is an inadequate means of protecting land or property ownership. Property and/or land ownership is profoundly political and legal 'obstacles' to the political will to expropriate and acquire land may be nothing more than a temporary irritant. It is in this context that any future undertaking for the protection of property in South Africa should be considered. It is in the light of this African experience that the ANC's proposals regarding property should be examined.

The ANC's draft proposal set out the principles of land

---

46. Ng'ong'ola, above, n. 10 p. 134.
47. Ng'ong'ola, above, n. 10 p. 135.

expropriation rather than the protection of property. The phraseology is familiar and similar to that which can be found in Bills of Rights provisions elsewhere in Africa.[48] On close examination the ANC proposals offer no firm protection for property rights (which include land). The protection ostensibly offered in clause 11.7 is immediately made subject to several caveats, some of which are contained in clause 11.7 itself. Clause 11.7 states that 'No person or legal entities shall be deprived of their possessions *except on grounds of public interest or public utility*, including the achievement of the objectives of the Constitution' (my italics). Further derogations from property protection are contained in clauses 11.5 and 11.11. The former allows the State to pass legislation to overcome past discrimination in relation to property rights and the latter is a general 'catch-all' provision. Any government needs powers to expropriate property where the general interest, public utility, or environmental needs have to be satisfied. If this is the case, is there any point in providing for the protection of property rights in a Bill of Rights? It would seem that the point of including property rights within a Bill of Rights is that these rights will be justiciable and subject to independent supervision. Yet this assumption should not be made too readily. Zambia, Zimbabwe and Malawi have all removed the jurisdiction of the courts from land acquisition/compensation disputes. This was done in order to avoid possible friction between the executive and judiciary.[49] The ANC proposals are silent as regards this specific point.

Clause 11.5 specifically considers the redress of past statutory discrimination *in relation to enjoyment of property rights* (my italics). If an emphasis is placed on the word 'enjoyment' of property rights, then it may be possible to enhance enjoyment of property rights without significantly affecting rights of property ownership. In this regard there may be considerable scope for the evolution of more 'non-ownership' property rights. If this is possible then the proposals may offer some protection to property owners. This approach would also allow scope for the ideas of property rights fragmentation as propounded by van der Walt.[50]

---

48. Ng'ong'ola, above, n. 10.
49. Ng'ong'ola, above, n. 10 p. 135.
50. Van der Walt, A.J. 'The fragmentation of land rights', *South African Journal of Human Rights* (1992) p. 431.

The Protection of Property in South Africa

While the ANC's constitutional proposals relating to property do not seem to provide assurance as regards property protection, they do set out general principles and seem to be imbued with a 'communal' spirit. Furthermore, property rights are profoundly political and can almost never be adequately protected by the law against the political will—nor should they.

The ANC proposals do seem to be more consistent with a customary view of property—that is, that it should be something people use and cannot own to the exclusion of others. This view is not inconsistent with the views put forward by the self-proclaimed 'superliberals'—the Critical Legal Scholars. Unger, their foremost spokesman, remarks as follows:[51]

> For one thing, our dominant conception of right imagines the right as a zone of discretion of the rightholder, a zone whose boundaries are more or less rigidly fixed at a time of the initial definition of the right. The right is a loaded gun that the rightholder may shoot at will in his corner of town. ...But the give-and-take of communal life and its characteristic concern for the actual effect of any decision upon the other are incompatible with this view of right and therefore if this is the only possible view, with any regime or rights.

If this interpretation of the ANC's proposals is correct its implementation will be interesting.

For the sake of convenience it may be said that the debate is dominated by two main groups. Firstly, by those who do not want property rights included in a future Bill of Rights and secondly, those who would include property rights in a Bill of Rights.

The most persuasive proponent of not including property rights within a Bill of Rights is Van der Walt. He argues for an evolutionary and diversified development of property rights. He talks of fragmentary rights of ownership which could be developed on a piecemeal societal basis but which would nevertheless be guided by a juridical form for the protection of these rights. He argues in particular for the retention and development of customary law approaches to property which he

---

51. Unger, Roberto Mangabeira, *The Critical Legal Studies Movement* (Harvard University Press, 1986), pp. 36-7.

argues would require protection.[52] He argues that the traditional first generation clauses protecting ownership will entrench the status quo. He is clearly incorrect in this interpretation as far as the ANC's proposal is concerned.

Those that prefer a Bill of Rights with first generation rights entrenched can be divided into several different groups. A common strand which runs through these proposals is a liberal rights thesis. While some of these commentators do not deal with the property issue specifically, they deal with it implicitly, arguing that the classical first generation (or civil and political) rights are of little use to those who suffer socio-economic deprivation. In order to participate adequately in the political process and have access to civil and political rights—such as freedom of speech, assembly and rights to property—it is necessary to empower these people through a substantive socio-economic programme of 'upliftment'. If this is not done then the entrenchment of first generation property rights will only serve to protect the 'rich'. Someone who can never afford any property hardly requires its protection. On this point most legal scholars are agreed. They differ, however, on what should be done to achieve the enfranchisement of those who are socio-economically deprived. Haysom[53] and Mureinik[54] have both argued that second generation or socio-economic rights ought to be entrenched in a future Bill of Rights. They differ on how these socio-economic rights ought to be implemented. Budlender[55] is less emphatic about the legal form of the socio-economic claims of the disenfranchised, while Davis[56] argues against the entrenchment of socio-economic rights in the constitution. While recognising the importance of socio-economic claims he prefers the concept of directive principles as the appropriate legal form for effectively realising these claims.

---

52. Above, n. 50.
53. Haysom, N. 'Constitutionalism, majoritarian democracy and socio-economic rights', *South African Journal of Human Rights* (1992), p. 451.
54. Mureinik, E. 'Beyond a charter of luxuries: Economic rights in the constitution', *South African Journal of Human Rights* (1992), p. 464.
55. Budlender, G. `The right to equitable access to land' *South African Journal of Human Rights* (1992), p. 295.
56. Davis, D. 'The case against the inclusion of socio-economic demands in a Bill of Rights except as directive principles', *South African Journal of Human Rights* (1992), p. 475.

The Protection of Property in South Africa

Haysom argues that a Bill of Rights should include socio-economic rights and that these should be treated on the same basis as civil and political (first generation) rights. To do less, or to exclude socio-economic rights such as the right to nutrition and shelter, would send the wrong message to the disenfranchised: namely, that these important substantive issues are less important and not worthy of the same protection as civil and political rights.[57] Haysom is aware of the fact that the enforcement of socio-economic rights are more problematical than civil and political rights. The reason being that the former tend to impose a positive duty on government to provide these amenities of life, whereas the former tend to place a negative obligation on government not to dilute or intrude upon protected rights. Another difficulty with socio-economic rights is the question of adjudication—placing the courts on a potential collision course with the Government over government policy. This difficulty Haysom clearly recognises for he proposes that where a Bill of Rights entrenches socio-economic rights it should only do so in terms of a general framework allowing the Government some room for movement.[58] Haysom is aware that only those socio-economic rights which the State can afford should be protected in a Bill of Rights and this explains his preference for 'framework' rights.[59]

There are several difficulties with the Haysom proposals. First, most Bills of Rights tend to be about a framework of general principles requiring substantial jurisprudential exposition and development through judicial interpretation. It is difficult to see how different Haysom's 'framework' of socio-economic rights would look in a constitution from the usual formulations. It would seem that he wants both to protect a political agenda constitutionally and at the same time allow a future government adequate scope to deal with these issues within the available resources. In this regard his proposals are uncertain. A second objection is his obsession with trying to construct an adequate liberal rights discourse within the South African context. This discourse relies heavily on judicial review, although Haysom proposes that such a review of socio-economic policy can be overseen by administrative agencies.[60] This argument, it would seem, still does

---

57. Haysom, above, n. 4, p.460-461.
58. *Ibid.*
59. *Ibid.*

not negate the need for judicial review of the decisions of those administrative agencies. The dangers of exposing the Government to constant judicial review on issues of Government policy have been recognised and avoided by other African states through the exclusion of judicial review.[61] It is not clear whether this is what Haysom is really proposing.

Mureinik's proposal is not dissimilar from that of Haysom. He argues that socio-economic claims should be recognised as rights within a Bill of Rights and be adequately protected by the courts through judicial review. While Haysom is less clear about the remedies and their enforcement in the sphere of socio-economic rights, Mureinik is quite explicit about the supervisory role of the courts. But his proposal has a nuance, namely, that the nature of judicial supervision of socio-economic rights would be less rigorous than civil and political rights. The review function of the court would be limited to ascertaining whether the Government has done its best to comply with the implementation of these socio-economic rights within the resource constraints.[62] The difficulties of the Mureinik approach is aptly illustrated by Davis:

> A constitution provides for a right to life, shelter and subsistence for all citizens. Mureinik suggests that were a court to be confronted with a constitutional dispute in which the annual national budget allocated considerable sums of money to the building of submarines rather than the prevention of starvation and the provision of shelter, a court would inevitably strike down that aspect of the budget as being in contravention of the state's obligation to provide shelter and subsistence. But would it? Assume, instead of Dworkin and Mureinik JJ, the court consisted of Milton Friedman and Leon Louw JJ. These judges would doubtless argue that money devoted to the building of submarines will give rise to a multiplier effect, the creation of a range of industries in a particular area, greater number of jobs and the consequent prevention of starvation. Mureinik's conclusion relies upon a specific world view of a particular community with one coherent philosophy all of which might be deemed

---

60. Haysom, above, n. 4, p. 459.
61. Ng'ong'ola, above, n. 10.
62. Mureinik, above, n. 54 p.471 *et seq.*

desirable but not inevitable given the flexibility of judicial performance and the plasticity of legal discourse.⁶³

Mureinik's proposals would, it is submitted, complicate the relationship between the judiciary and government of the day, serving as a veto on government policy. It is unlikely that any future government would want its credibility and legitimacy continually subjected to judicial scrutiny. A further objection to this approach, as Davis notes, is that it is likely to undermine civil and political society by removing politics to the courts thereby weakening the democratic processes.⁶⁴

Davis treats socio-economic or second generation rights differently as directive principles. This idea has been lifted from the Indian constitution and seems to depend for its effectiveness on a particularly activist court. Directive principles set out societal goals but lack the 'bite' of first generation rights—the basic political freedoms. Directive principles, according to Davis, serve to provide recognition of social and economic rights and allow for meaningful democratic participation. However, Davis concedes that directive principles straddle the divide between rights and politics and are therefore more difficult to enforce constitutionally than is the case of first generation rights. He advocates that these directive principles of state policy provide an interpretative framework for an 'honest constitutional process of transformation'.⁶⁵

There are also those who would do without directive principles and only wish to see the first generation rights enforced.⁶⁶

It is far from clear just how these directive principles are supposed to work when it comes to the practical problem of land redistribution. One criticism, which is equally applicable to directive principles, is an over-reliance on the judiciary as some sort of impartial arbiter that might be able to resolve what politicians are not prepared to tackle. The same criticism Davis made against the inclusion of socio-economic rights within a Bill of Rights may be levelled against his proposal of directive principles. It would be up to the court to apply these principles when it deems it necessary and fit to do so. Perhaps the

---

63. Davis, above, n. 56 p. 484.
64. *Ibid.* p. 488 *et seq.*
65. Davis, above, n. 56.
66. Lewis, C. 'The right of private property in a new political dispensation in South Africa', *South African Journal of Human Rights* (1992), p. 389.

argument for directive principles is that it will shift the role of the judiciary to discretion of application (of these principles) rather than discretion in interpretation (of socio-economic rights).

Budlender,[67] in my view, has stated[68] the problems regarding property most succinctly:

> And so the central issue emerges. Yes, of course we need property rights. Property should be a right. But most of the property rights debate centres on the right of those who hold property, to retain it. What is missing is a serious discussion of the right of the property-less to what they need for a decent life—because that, too, should be understood as a property right.

He proposes a Bill of Rights which will contain a provision placing the Government under a duty to make suitable land and housing available to the landless and homeless. Furthermore the constitution should provide adequate means of ensuring implementation of this proposal and provide for a tribunal with appropriate powers to deal with land and housing claims.

The precise legal form of these proposals—whether it is by directive principle or entrenched right—is less important, as long as it is effective. Budlender's first point is covered by the ANC proposals as is his plea for affirmative action for home and land provision. Land/property must be, according to Budlender, redistributed without just compensation as this will be too expensive for any South African government.[69]

Budlender's approach comes closest to the pattern of land acquisition and distribution of Zambia, Zimbabwe and Malawi discussed previously. He is clear[70] about the fact that the only way to—

> achieve a true balance between the rights of property-holders and property-less is to weaken existing property rights, as a matter of deliberate policy. Whether that should be done is a question not of constitutional principle, but political power and priorities.

---

67. Budlender, above, n. 55.
68. Budlender, above, n. 55 p. 299.
69. Budlender, above, n. 55 p. 303.
70. Budlender, above, n. 55 p. 304.

Budlender, therefore, realises that the issue of property, more particularly land, is profoundly political. The recognition of rights to property is always indeterminate in this sense that it is never certain or fixed. Notions of property and rights to property are flexible. The ANC proposals seem to accommodate Budlender's approach to the property question.

4 CRITIQUE

One important aspect which characterizes the current debate in South Africa concerning a Bill of Rights is the importance attached to the juridification process of essentially contentious political issues. The usual uncritical liberal paradigm has been adopted as some kind of panacea for a political problem: *deus ex machina*. Although liberal academe has been generally critical of the South African judiciary for not adequately protecting basic civil liberties, there is now a preparedness to entrust them with even more responsibility than before. There is almost an optimistic instrumentalist, and deterministic, approach to the Bill of Rights issue—an excessive confidence on the quality and degree of judicial performance—yet little evidence is produced which gives cause for such optimism.

Although Bophutatswana was one of the former South African regime's independent Homelands the experiment with a Bill of Rights there has on the whole been unfortunate. The Bill was initially enthusiastically received and served a useful ideological function, yet as time passed little credence was given to its basic first generation rights provisions.[71] Ever since Hiemstra CJ's pronouncement in *Smith* v. *Attorney-General, Bophutatswana:*

> The Court helps to shape the Declaration of Human Rights with great deference to the Legislature. A Court which is over-active in striking down legislation can destroy the exalted instrument it is trying to bring to life, it can incur the resentment of the Legislature and cause the Declaration, which was meant to be a charter of freedom, to become a clog upon the wheels of government. That must be avoided

---

71. See *Monakale and others* v. *Government of the Republic of Boputhatswana and Others*, 1991 (1) SALR 598 BGD.

for the sake of the Constitution itself and for the sake of the stature of parliament as the highest law-making forum of the nation...[72]

The examples of Zambia and Zimbabwe show that the issue of the protection of property, especially land ownership, is a profoundly public issue and cannot be divorced from socio-economic, and above all, political imperatives. It is the latter, rather than judicial pronouncements, that will have a decisive influence on the basis of land ownership in a future South Africa. Budlender aptly comments:

> Claims to land come down in the end to decisions about land use and availability, and about how society's resources are to be applied. The questions raised by land claims are thus highly political—not in the party-political sense, but in the more fundamental sense that, in Laswell's famous phrase, they are about who gets what, when and how. The decisions are usually made in the administrative system, by officials of local, regional and national government.[73]

5 CONCLUSION

Whether the Bill of Rights ought to be the product of a process or whether it should initiate a process goes to the heart of the law enterprise, and there probably will not be any agreement on it.

Budlender's comment requires context—that is the context in which government will make what decision and how. What is clear is the fact that there will be considerable constraints on any future government. The most important constraint will be the constantly shrinking South African economy.[74] During the three years after 1990 there was a negative growth rate. Unemployment in 1993 was estimated at 40 per cent of the economically active population.[75] A new government will have not only to stop this trend but also to reverse it. This means restoring confidence and ending the violence.[76] In this regard it may be

---

72. 1984 (1) SALR 196 B.
73. Budlender, above, n. 55 p. 303.
74. *The Star* 14 August 1992.
75. *Business Day* 7th August 1992; *The Star* 19th August 1992.
76. BBC1, 1st October, 1993. Nelson Mandela remarked that as long as unemployment remains high crime was likely to remain high. Crime would only decrease when more jobs are created.

that a new government will restore legitimacy, but obedience to the law may take much longer to restore. For a government which hopes to provide a legal basis for its actions, the restoration of the legal infrastructure is an urgent priority. All this suggests that the new government will have its hands full trying to run the country.

A programme of land reform is, in my view, essential for the successful outcome of some of the issues listed above.

It seems unlikely that a new government will introduce radical changes in the law and it is likely that the land reform programme will be proceeded with on a piecemeal basis. If this is the case then the issue of access to land will be important. It may be possible to redistribute some agricultural land since 28 per cent of South Africa's commercial farmers provide 74 per cent of all agricultural produce.[77] In particular the wine industry is one of the greatest agricultural successes in South Africa not requiring a state subsidy. A modest solution in this direction could be achieved by either ending or changing the basis for agricultural subsidies so that, through the usual judicial procedures for insolvency, a significant amount of agricultural land may be acquired for the purpose of redistribution. There is already evidence to suggest that this is likely to happen soon. The State has for some time diverted funds previously allocated to agriculture towards a social fund.[78] While this proposal will yield very modest results the value of its ideological impact should not be dismissed.

Of greater significance, perhaps, is how property rights may be protected in a new South Africa. While I think it is likely that a government will adopt a piecemeal approach, it should strive to relocate property rights within the concept of community or public interest. This means that the 'right' a person has in property will be determined within a context of community values. This is the argument essentially made by Unger.[79] It means that the rights of an individual should be found in the values underpinning a particular community or society. 'Rights' ought not to be regarded as something to be asserted against others in opposition to community interests. This approach will not only accord with traditional African values, where access to land

---

77. Hansard, 20th March 1991, col 3343-3344.
78. Hansard, 20th March 1991, col 3335 *et seq.*
79. Unger, above, n. 51.

becomes more important than having dominium over it, but need not be inconsistent with progressive liberal values. This process is likely to be evolutionary rather than revolutionary.

The protection of property always takes place within a political or communal context. The right to property—the ability of one person to exclude another from access to or the enjoyment of that property—is always contingent on other factors, be they socio-economic or political. In this regard South Africa is no exception. Yet there may be additional factors which may prolong the present protection afforded to property in South Africa. These other factors include the need to restore the economic fortunes of the country, or at least staunch the decline. The International Monetary Fund (IMF) is likely to impose an economic regime on a new South African government as the IMF has done in other African countries. This is an additional factor which leads to the conclusion that the land issue is likely to be dealt with on a piecemeal basis.

It has been argued that a Bill of Rights cannot of itself protect the right to property, unless the culture or values of the society sustains such protection. The law of itself does not offer protection or guarantee rights.

Chapter Six

Legislating for Peace: An Overview of Attempts to Promote Peace in South Africa

J. R. Midgley

1 BACKGROUND

South African State President F. W. De Klerk called a peace conference on 24 May 1991, but the African National Congress (ANC), the Pan Africanist Congress (PAC) and the South African Council of Churches failed to attend. Thereafter a 'continuation committee' convened a closed meeting which attracted delegates from across the political spectrum, with the exception of the right-wing groups. Five working groups were formed to investigate key issues and these reported to a Preparatory Committee of the National Peace Initiative.

Churches and the business community then brokered the National Peace Accord, which was signed on 14 September 1991 by thirty-six parties, governments and organisations. Right-wing groups again boycotted the meeting, while the PAC and AZAPO participated in the proceedings but did not sign the Accord. The aim of the signatories was to signify a common purpose in bringing about an end to political violence in the country. They agreed upon codes of conduct for political parties and the security forces as well as upon guidelines for community reconstruction and development. They also agreed to establish mechanisms for implementing the Accord. In particular, chapter 7 of the Accord provided for the establishment of a National Secretariat which would establish and coordinate Regional and Local Dispute Resolution Committees. (In December 1992 it was decided to call dispute resolution committees 'peace committees', and although neither the Accord nor the legislation was amended to reflect this change, the new nomenclature will be used in this paper.)

On 20 September 1991 an interim National Peace Committee was formed and during December the first peace committees were established in Natal and Soweto.

The Internal Peace Institutions Act[1] was passed in June 1992, and gave statutory recognition to some of the Peace Accord's provisions. The legislation was put into effect on 4 November 1992 although the Act was still not fully operational since the regulations which were to give effect to the Act's intention had not yet been promulgated. Much of the statute's value would rest on the nature of these regulations.

As was pointed out in Parliament,[2] the Act was the first product of multilateral negotiations to be enacted as law and even though it was passed by an unrepresentative Parliament, it was the first statute which purported to reflect the considered opinions of a substantial portion of disenfranchised South Africans. However, despite its commendable pedigree, the Act was not necessarily an ideal model for the future regulation of society's affairs. While it aimed to enable representative structures to participate in establishing and maintaining peace—in other words, to promote democratic grassroots participation in the regulation of society—the management model and style belonged to a dying era, a 'top-down' system whereby participants in the process were appointed by a higher authority with whom responsibility lay.

This paper deals with the structures which were established to give effect to the provisions of the National Peace Accord. It describes the powers and duties of the institutions and the type of issue with which they became involved. The paper also looks at the tensions inherent in the system and the need for a return to the management model envisaged in the Accord.

---

1.   135 of 1992.
2.   By H. J. Bester: Hansard 16 June 1992 col. 11332.

Legislating for Peace

2 THE NATIONAL PEACEKEEPING STRUCTURE

The Peace Accord, which has a preamble and ten chapters, is at the heart of the structure. The first chapter sets out principles; the next three contain codes of conduct for political parties and security forces; chapter five addresses socio-economic reconstruction issues; chapter six deals with what has become known as the Goldstone Commission, that is, the Commission of Inquiry Regarding the Prevention of Public Violence and Intimidation; chapter seven deals with community participation, in the form of the National Peace Secretariat and peace committees; chapter eight establishes a National Peace Committee; chapter nine with the enforcement of the Accord, and chapter ten makes provision for special criminal courts.

The following statement summarises the nature of the structure:[3]

> The National Peace Accord is based on three main pillars, each of which has a unique function, separate from but complementary to the others.
>
> The National Peace Committee supervises the peace process as set out in the Peace Accord, publicises it and applies the code of conduct for political parties.
>
> The Commission of Inquiry into the Prevention of Public Violence and Intimidation investigates the phenomenon of public violence and intimidation and exposes the background to it and the reasons for it. The process is similar to a judicial process and the members of the Commission are jurists.
>
> The National Peace Secretariat has the task, by means of the various dispute resolution committees, of preventing future violence through mediation and facilitation. The Secretariat and the committees have a political basis and can therefore not undertake any investigation into past violence, nor can they make findings on past violence or express any judgment on who was responsible for the violence.

---

3. National Peace Secretariat's report of 24 April 1992.

Negotiating Justice

Figure 1 illustrates the structure:

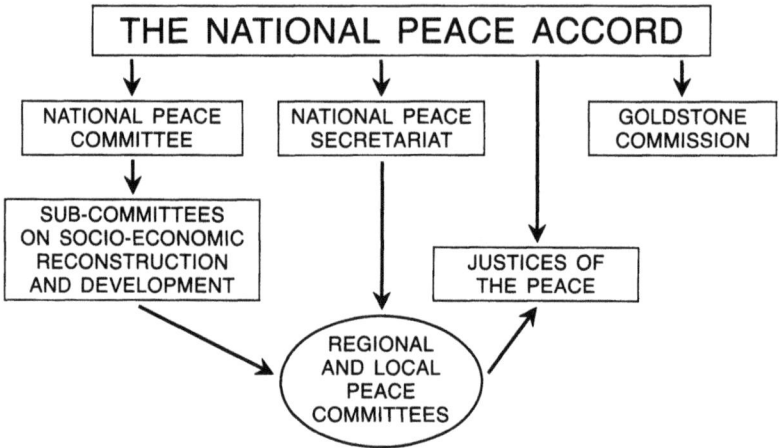

Fig. 1. *The Structures Established by the National Peace Accord.*

The Commission and the Secretariat are therefore not subcommittees of the National Peace Committee—they are independent statutory bodies working in conjunction with the National Peace Committee. Contact between these structures is informal, but the chairperson of the Secretariat is a member of the Executive Committee of the National Peace Committee.

2.1 The National Peace Committee

The National Peace Committee (NPC) is the *de facto* umbrella organisation. It is a non-statutory institution which draws its members from the political parties and organisations represented on the Accord's preparatory committee. The NPC may draw additional members from other signatory parties where it believes that such inclusion will give effect to the Accord.[4] Its objective is to monitor and make recommendations on the implementation of the Accord and to ensure

---

4. Clause 8.1.1 of the Accord.

compliance with the codes of conduct.[5] It can, amongst others, decide or resolve disputes and recommend legislation.[6]

By mid-1993 the NPC had undertaken a number of tasks. It had facilitated the establishment of the Secretariat and structures had been set up to monitor the South African Police and the South African Defence Force. A Police Board, consisting of representatives from the police and ten members of the public, was formed on 27 April 1992. The NPC was investigating issues such as the composition of the police force, clandestine and covert operations, a code of conduct for the defence force, dangerous weapons and self-protection units and would possibly in future make recommendations to the Minister of Law and Order on the training and efficient functioning of the police. The NPC was also charged with establishing special criminal courts to deal with unrest-related cases and cases involving public violence and intimidation, but the idea was subsequently shelved. It was felt that there was a negative connotation associated with special courts, and instead legislation was introduced to create special procedures to deal with public violence cases. The marketing of the Accord was delegated to the National Peace Secretariat, but the NPC still dealt with complaints about breaches of the Peace Accord. The National Complaints Investigation Commission had by July received 162 complaints about breaches, arising mainly out of the codes of conduct. Dossiers were prepared and a team of lawyers attempted to settle the issues to avoid sending complaints to arbitrators.

The Peace Accord recognises that reconstruction and development are conditions precedent for peace and the reduction of violence. The NPC was responsible for socio-economic reconstruction and in some regions sub-committees were installed to launch programmes. Subsequently all Regional Peace Committees were instructed to employ coordinators for socio-economic reconstruction and development. Once installed these structures facilitated the development of economic and human resources of communities and initiated reconstruction projects. However, until these coordinators were in place Local and Regional Peace Committees had to promote this work in addition to their regular functions.

---

5. Clause 8.2.
6. Clause 8.3.

Development agencies expressed concern that the peace structures might become yet another funding forum or development agency, but the NPC was sensitive to this issue. While it had established the Peace Accord Trust and raised funds from non-government sources which could be channelled into projects, the NPC's main aim, after identifying potential flash points, was to assist communities raising funds from other agencies. The NPC concentrated on reconstruction projects that would facilitate peace and defuse violence. For example, in the Wits/Vaal region some fifty hostels were identified as flash points and, with the NPC's facilitation, funds became available to upgrade some of them. My own experience in this area also serves to illustrate the procedure. During a mediation between a community delegation and the police, inadequate policing was identified as a major source of friction. The parties appointed a commission to investigate how policing methods in Grahamstown could be improved. The commission contacted the Peace Committee and the NPC and drew up a funding proposal in conjunction with the NPC. The NPC then approached a potential donor and secured funds for the project.

2.2 The Commission of Inquiry for the Prevention of Public Violence and Intimidation

This commission, universally known as the Goldstone Commission, was appointed in terms of the Prevention of Public Violence and Intimidation Act[7] which came into operation on 17 July 1991. The signatories of the Accord felt that the Commission of Inquiry could be used as an instrument to investigate and expose the background and reasons for violence.[8] The Commission was appointed on 24 October 1991 and held its inaugural meeting on 28 and 29 October.

The Commission was headed by Mr. Justice Goldstone who was assisted by five commissioners. The aim of the Commission was to inquire into cases of violence and intimidation, to find out the nature and causes thereof and to determine who was involved. It could also inquire into any steps that should be taken to prevent public violence and intimidation and make recommendations to the State President on

---

7.   139 of 1991.
8.   Clause 6.3.

Legislating for Peace

how to stop violence. In September 1992 five special investigation units—consisting of twenty-six advocates, attorneys, policemen and defence force members and based in Cape Town, Durban, Johannesburg, Port Elizabeth and East London, and Pietermaritzburg—were formed to assist the Commission in probing violence.

The first reports dealt with train violence, hostels, the Bisho massacre, conduct of the SAP in the Vaal Triangle area, RENAMO soldiers in kwaZulu, violence at Mooi River, Natal and the President Steyn Gold Mine in Welkom, the conduct of 32 Battalion in Phola Park, the taxi industries in the Western Cape, Ivory Park and Alexandra and the Thokoza violence. The Commission also reported on the regulation of gatherings and it also submitted a draft Bill on the topic to Parliament.

2.3 The National Peace Secretariat

2.3.1 Structure

The National Peace Secretariat (the Secretariat) was established in November 1991 and operated from Pretoria. Originally it had seven members who, apart from its chairperson and a representative of the Department of Justice, were all active participants in the national political arena. Subsequently, the Internal Peace Institutions Act enabled the Secretariat to be established as a statutory body. The Act provided that the Secretariat would consist of the Executive Director of the Internal Peace Institutions, no more than two persons appointed by the State President at his discretion and up to six members appointed by the State President from a list of ten names submitted by the NPC.[9] In fact two representatives from each of the ANC, the IFP and the National Party were appointed. The latter group of persons served for a period of three years, but could be reappointed. No mention was made of the tenure of the other members. After consulting the NPC, the State President could terminate a member's appointment on the following grounds: misconduct, continued ill-health, incapacity to carry out duties effectively, or at the member's request.[10] Vacancies could be

---

9. Section 3(1).
10. Section 3(5).

filled.[11] Membership was restricted to South African citizens permanently resident in the country.[12]

The Secretariat was responsible for establishing Regional Peace Committees and assisted in the formation of Local Peace Committees.[13] It also coordinated and monitored their activities[14] and had to submit, at least once every six months, a report on the extent of its supervision to the State President[15] and, within fourteen days thereafter, to the Goldstone Commission and the NPC.[16] The report would be tabled in Parliament.[17] If it so wished, the Secretariat could inform the Goldstone Commission of issues surrounding occurrences of violence and intimidation, including steps which peace committees had taken.

The Secretariat also had the power to appoint subcommittees, the membership of which was not necessarily confined to Secretariat members, to assist it in its tasks.[18] Training, publicity, research and data collection, socio-economic reconstruction, marketing and monitoring subcommittees were established and permission was given to establish operations centres at major violence flash points around the country. The Secretariat could also use the services of competent persons, and remunerate them, to achieve its purposes.[19] Facilitators were used to overcome distrust and hostility in some areas in order to prepare the climate for the formation of peace committees. So, too, professional trainers were used to teach persons the necessary skills.

The Secretariat determined its own procedural rules,[20] except that relating to a quorum,[21] which was formed by the majority of the Secretariat's members, and decision-making, which is by consensus.[22]

There was some indication that the previous non-statutory Secretariat was not entirely happy with these legislative provisions, although its difficulties were not set out in detail. Subsequent

---

11. Section 3(6).
12. section 3(4).
13. Sections 4(a) and 4(b).
14. Section 4(c).
15. Section 6(1).
16. Section 6(3).
17. Section 6(4).
18. Section 4(f).
19. Section 4(e).
20. Section 5(5).
21. Section 5(2).
22. Section 5(4).

documents indicated that the dissatisfaction may have stemmed from the ANC constituency which did not accept certain provisions. For a while the ANC refused to nominate a member to the Secretariat because it did not accept the clause allowing the State President to appoint two members to the executive. The provisions were also criticised by, amongst others, Dr John Lamola, Head of the Justice and Social Ministries Department of the South African Council of Churches.[23]

The gravamen of the objections appears to have been that the statutory structure did not correspond to that set out in the Peace Accord, namely, that the Secretariat would consist of at least four persons nominated by the NPC, one representative of the Department of Justice and no more than four appointed members. The provision allowing the State President to select two members according to his discretion[24] also came under fire. Although the State President had apparently given the assurance that the spirit of the Peace Accord would not be violated when appointments were made, and had in fact appointed members solely from a list nominated by the previous Secretariat, Lamola's criticisms were valid. These were: that the government of the day had been made 'the guardian and guarantor of the Peace Accord'; that the State President (not the NPC or the Goldstone Commission) was 'the virtual patron and commander-in-chief of the National Peace Accord and its structures', having the capacity to require reports and being the person to whom the Secretariat reports; and that the State President's powers of appointment and dismissal were too extensive.[25]

2.3.2 Activities

The Secretariat was involved in a variety of activities. It mediated the dispute between Paul Simon and the PAC and AZAPO (who were not signatories of the Accord) when threats were made to disrupt Simon's tour. This led to a public undertaking to refrain from expressing violent

---

23. Lamola, J. 'Internal Peace Institutions Act: Base or Grave of the National Peace Accord?' 18 August 1992.
24. Section 3(1)(a).
25. See Lamola, above n. 23.

Negotiating Justice

opposition to the tour. The Secretariat also took an active part in trying to end the violence in the Natal region and met with Ciskei leaders in attempts to involve them in the peace process.

In Soweto and Phalaborwa the Secretariat chairperson, Antonie Gildenhuys, initially chaired meetings of the local peace committees because the members could not agree on the appointment of a chairperson. Members of the Secretariat have acted on occasion as observers at political marches and rallies which seems to have had a calming effect on most crowds. Gildenhuys has also conducted extensive negotiations with the leaders of Bophutatswana, Ciskei and kwaZulu on matters relating to free political activity in these areas.

Marketing was identified as a priority. The aim was to promote the work of the peace structures so that people at grassroots level could become aware of the presence of peace committees and how to make use of the facilities to prevent violence.

The training sub-committee put together panels of trainers and process observers. A training model and resource materials were prepared so that quality consistency could be maintained. Training was concentrated on sessions for members of the Peace Committees.

Although a number of independent monitoring groups existed, monitoring remained one of the more important tasks of the peace structures. It had a specific and complementary role in the pursuit of peace. In placing the behaviour of people under the spotlight, monitoring encouraged self-discipline. The Secretariat had a monitoring subcommittee which worked in close association with other monitoring structures.

2.4 The Directorate: Internal Peace Institutions

This Directorate was subject to the control and direction of the Minister of Justice,[26] but would in future fall under the Minister of Home Affairs. An Executive Director was responsible for its daily administration and was assisted by a team of public servants. The Secretariat was, in July 1993, served by twenty-one permanent employees at its Head Office in Pretoria and thirty-five at regional and local level. The Directorate had to submit an annual report to the

---

26. Section 7(2).

Legislating for Peace

Minister of Justice who would then table the report in Parliament. The Directorate was responsible for performing the administrative duties of the Secretariat and the peace committees.[27] On the recommendation of any of these committees the Directorate could appoint personnel for those particular committees.[28] The Directorate also exercised control over the finances which Parliament assigned to these structures,[29] although independently-donated funds were under the direct control of the Secretariat.

The lack of adequate infrastructure hampered peace committee activities. The Secretariat had no budget for a long time and received funds through the Department of Justice. In some instances organisations like the Independent Mediation Services of South Africa (IMSSA) and the Consultative Business Movement (CBM) provided secretarial services. Initially the infrastructure in the regions was provided by the South African Communication Services, the governmental publicity agency, but only two regions continued to make use of this facility, for as it was a government body it was not generally acceptable to the communities. Permanent staff were appointed throughout the country, both at regional and local level, and separate offices were rented.

2.5 Peace Committees

2.5.1 Introduction

The Peace Accord required that disputes should be settled by using simple and expeditious procedures and that participation of the parties to the dispute were essential. 'Proven methods of mediation, arbitration and adjudication' were suggested.[30] *Mediation* is a mechanism for facilitating agreement between parties and involves the intervention of one or more facilitators with no stake in the dispute. Parties must voluntarily agree to the process and the facilitators should be independent and impartial. Other important features are the maintenance of confidentiality and procedural flexibility. The dispute is

---

27. Section 9(1)(a).
28. Section 9(2).
29. Section 9(1)(c).
30. Clause 1.12.

resolved by the parties themselves with the aid of the facilitator/s. *Arbitration*, on the other hand, is a process whereby a dispute is referred by the parties to a person or persons of their own choosing, called an arbitrator, who holds a private enquiry in a judicial manner and whose decision is final and binding upon the parties. Again, the process is voluntary and like mediation, additional to the judicial process. It is not clear what is meant by the term '*adjudication*'. It can refer to other forms of alternative dispute resolution, such as 'medarb', or 'armed', or to administrative-type decision making.[31] Either way, it excludes the judicial process.

As will be seen below, Regional Peace Committees (RPCs) and Local Peace Committees (LPCs) were formed throughout the country and, like the Secretariat, these committees received statutory recognition. The Internal Peace Institutions Act provided for the establishment of RPCs and LPCs and set out their objects:[32]

> A regional committee or local committee shall *as the representative of the community in the region or area* in respect of which that committee has been established, strive to terminate, combat or prevent public violence and intimidation by means of negotiation.

The value of such an objects clause was that it served as a standard against which the conduct of peace committees could be tested. However, it was not only the objects of the Internal Peace Institutions Act which needed to be realised, but also those of the Prevention of Public Violence and Intimidation Act and chapter 7 of the National Peace Accord.

2.5.2 Regional Peace Committees

Eleven Regional Peace Committees were established by the National Secretariat in the following regions: Natal-kwaZulu, Border-Ciskei, Wits-Vaal, Western Cape, Orange Free State, Northern Cape, Far Northern Transvaal, Northern Transvaal, Eastern Transvaal, Eastern Cape and Western Transvaal (see Figure 2):

---

31. Section 11. The italics are mine.
32. Section 12(2)(a).

CLASSIFICATION OF REGIONS

1. Natal / kwaZulu
2. Ciskei / Border
3. Witwatersrand / Vaal
4. Orange Free State
5. Western Cape
6. Northern Transvaal
7. Far Northern Transvaal
8. Eastern Transvaal
9. Western Transvaal
10. Northern Cape
11. Eastern Cape

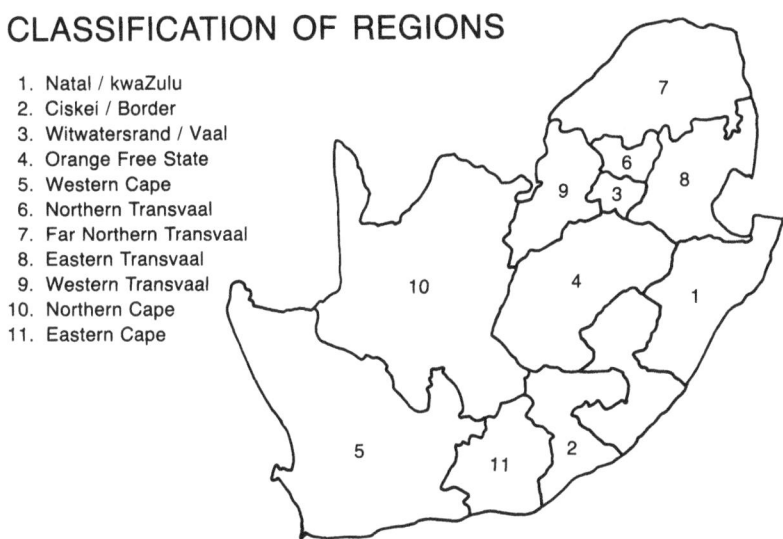

Fig. 2. *Regions of the Peace Committees.*

There was no limit to the number of members on the committees. The only qualification necessary to serve on a committee was that a person must, in the opinion of the Secretariat, be able to make a contribution to the performance of the committee's functions.[33] The Secretariat would also determine the length of tenure, but members were eligible for reappointment.[34] Members were not remunerated but travelling and subsistence expenses could be claimed. Members could

---

33. Section 12(3)(a).
34. Section 12(3)(b).

be dismissed from office where the Secretariat believed that there was a valid reason for doing so.[35]

```
┌─────────────────────────────────┐
│         REGIONAL                │
│  DISPUTE RESOLUTION COMMITTEE   │
│         FUNCTIONS               │
└─────────────────────────────────┘
```

— MAINTAIN EFFECTIVE REGIONAL AND LOCAL PEACE STRUCTURES

— ESTABLISH LOCAL DISPUTE RESOLUTION COMMITTEES

— SETTLE DISPUTES AND MONITOR AGREEMENTS

— APPOINT JUSTICES OF THE PEACE

— OVERSEE TRAINING OF PEACE COMMITTEE MEMBERS IN NEGOTIATION AND MEDIATION SKILLS

— ESTABLISH AND OVERSEE COMMITTEE ON SOCIO-ECONOMIC RECONSTRUCTION AND DEVELOPMENT

Fig. 3. *Functions of the Regional Dispute Resolution Committees.*

Once established, an RPC determined its own meeting procedure,[36] except that decisions had to be reached by consensus,[37] and it could appoint an executive and any other sub-committee to assist it.[38] It had to carry out the orders of the Secretariat.[39] In addition, RPCs were empowered to supervise the activities of LPCs and every three months, or when requested to do so, they had to report on LPC activities to the

---

35. Section 12(2(c).
36. Section 12(2)(e).
37. Section 12(2)(d).
38. Section 13.
39. Section 16(1).

Secretariat.[40] Any matter of interest to the Secretariat had also to be reported to it.[41]

2.5.3 Local Peace Committees

Local Peace Committees were constituted by appointing representatives reflecting the institutions and needs of the community. Initially LPCs gained their legitimacy by representing the people in the community.

LOCAL DISPUTE RESOLUTION COMMITTEE FUNCTIONS

– MUST REPRESENT A WIDE SPECTRUM OF COMMUNITY

– FACILITATE THE DEVELOPMENT OF TRUST AMONGST THE VARIOUS PARTIES

– SETTLE DISPUTES AT GRASSROOTS LEVEL

– MONITOR POTENTIAL FLASHPOINTS AND TAKE STEPS TO DEAL WITH THEM PROACTIVELY

– PROMOTE COMPLIANCE WITH THE PEACE ACCORD

– ENSURE THAT CODES OF CONDUCT ARE ADHERED TO

Fig. 4. *Functions of the Local Dispute Resolution Committees.*

By the end of July 1992, thirty-eight LPCs had been appointed throughout the country, while twenty-one committees were in the

---

40. Section 16(2).
41. Section 15 of the Act and clause 7.4.8 of the Accord.

process of being established. The count towards the end of August 1992 was thirty-nine established committees, three interim committees and fifty-five committees in formation. In November the Secretariat reported that fifty committees were fully operational, six were established but not functioning properly, or had disintegrated, while thirty local committees were in the process of establishment, with an additional twelve planned for the Natal/kwaZulu area. Committees were established at a rapid rate and towards the end of February 1993 eighty-five LPCs were in existence.

Amongst other duties, LPCs were to attend to matters referred to them by the RPCs and the Goldstone Commission, to create an atmosphere of trust and reconciliation, to cooperate with local Justices of the Peace in preventing violence and intimidation, to settle disputes through negotiation, to liaise with local police and magistrates and to agree upon rules relating to marches, gatherings and rallies.[42]

As to the jurisdiction of the LPCs, it appears that since they were set up to enforce the Peace Accord they should have confined themselves to the resolution of disputes arising out of transgressions of the codes of conduct adopted by signatories of the Accord. Nothing in that document indicated a wider jurisdiction, but in practice non-signatories and individuals did refer disputes to LPCs. Nonetheless, the Act eliminated this minor difficulty and LPCs were able to work among non-signatories as well.

In terms of the statute an RPC might establish any number of LPCs within its region, provided that the Secretariat agreed.[43] The Secretariat and the RPC also determined the size of a particular LPC and appointed its members.[44] The size of the committees varied: in some cases LPCs consisted of up to sixty members serving more than a million people in the Kempton Park local committee area for example. The RPC also determined the length of a local committee member's tenure and members were eligible for reappointment.[45] As in the case of members of the RPC, no remuneration was payable, but subsistence and travel expenses might be claimed. Members could be dismissed from office where the RPC believed that there was a valid reason for

---

42. Section 14(1).
43. Section 14(2)(a).
44. Section 14(3)(a).
45. Section 14(3)(b).

Legislating for Peace

doing so.[46]

Once established, the LPC determined its own meeting procedure,[47] except that decisions had to be reached by consensus.[48] It could appoint an executive to assist it.[49]

LPCs were obliged to carry out instructions from the Secretariat and the RPCs. However, they could also use their own initiative where they believed that peace in the community was threatened and that the issue could not be resolved by negotiation.[50] In such instances they had either to report the matter to an available Justice of the Peace or to the appropriate RPC and provide them with all the relevant information.[51] The Act made no mention of LPCs themselves resolving such problems before reporting them to other authorities, but it is suggested that they should be able to do so. This, after all, formed part of their function as set out in the Peace Accord, namely, to 'settle disputes causing public violence or intimidation, by negotiating with the parties concerned and recording the terms of such settlements'.

2.5.4 Activities of Peace Committees

In many instances peace committees functioned most satisfactorily, but in others, especially in Natal and the Border/Ciskei region, and also in some parts of the Transvaal, progress was hampered by political infighting and an unwillingness to acknowledge the right to existence of opposing political groups. The Ciskei Government, for example, withdrew from the Regional Peace Committee in March 1962, while the violence in Natal necessitated the appointment of two paid facilitators to assist with the establishment of committees and with their activities.

Much of the facilitation work related to marches and political demonstrations, and peace committees successfully diffused potentially violent situations in, amongst others, Schweizer-Reineke, Hertzogville, Potgietersrus, Krugersdorp and Bisho. Unfortunately, the

---

46. Section 14(1)(c).
47. Section 14(1)(e).
48. Section 14(1)(d).
49. Section 15(2).
50. *Ibid.*
51. 16 of 1963.

circumstances of the second Bisho march, where the Secretariat could not broker a settlement, is well known.

Amongst the successes were the activities of the interim crisis committee in Alexandra, which met on a daily basis at one stage to deal with the violence. Committees have also resolved taxi wars in the Western Cape, consumer boycotts in Pietersburg and Phalaborwa and squatter issues and hospital workers' strikes in the Transvaal. In Grahamstown they have dealt with such diverse issues as inadequate policing services, opposition to rates increases, poor quality municipal water, church disputes, taxi disputes, grazing cattle on municipal commonage, disputes between persons who have suffered forced removals and disputes between civic organisations and municipal councils. Although at first sight these issues often appeared to be civic issues, many cases had political overtones as political organisations jockeyed for position prior to the expected elections.

With one exception, all the Grahamstown disputes were settled peacefully. Other committees were not as fortunate. The violence in Natal is well known, and some committee members there lost their lives while performing this very important civic duty. The volunteer monitors of the Bisho march were also in enormous danger when they unexpectedly found themselves under fire from the Ciskei forces. And consider the contrast in two neighbouring areas in Transvaal, that of the Boksburg/Benoni Peace Committee and of the Germiston Peace Committee. The former area was quite peaceful with disputes mainly of a civic nature. Germiston, however, which has a large railway junction, was the scene of much of the reported train violence. There the chairperson of the Peace Committee was often called out in the early hours of the morning to deal with the violence that erupted on the station platforms.

Training in the skills required to resolve disputes that could give rise to political violence was essential for continuing success. It soon became apparent, as issues came to be referred to the Peace Committees, that members needed to become acquainted with the mediation process and that mediation-skills training was of vital importance.

One of the most positive outcomes was that a sizable police contingent attended the workshops which were subsequently set up by the Peace Committees. The interaction between the police and members of the public was most beneficial. In a sense this was one of the first steps in the healing process which has to take place. Relationships were

Legislating for Peace

established which have already paid dividends. When disputes occurred people who already knew each other dealt with the issues and the process became a lot easier to manage. The more that people—the police and members of the public—were exposed to each other's views, the greater the benefit to the entire community.

However, training should not be limited to Peace Committee members and a conscious effort should be made to provide skills throughout our society. Instead of limiting one's effort to the training of mediators, one should have a broader vision: to be proactive in training potential adversaries in negotiation and mediation processes with a view to changing the prevailing political culture from animosity and intolerance to joint problem-solving. The Grahamstown Peace Committee identified an enormous need for training in communities in our sub-region. Often conflicts arose or were exacerbated because people did not have skills to deal with issues. One of the Peace Committee's tasks should therefore be to make a training service available to people outside the peace structures. The true test, therefore, was to inculcate a non-adversarial ethos, and the skills required to implement it, in a community. In Grahamstown we intended preparing the ground with proposed pilot projects in selected local schools during August and September 1993. At first we intended concentrating on issues such as communication and listening skills and problem-solving methods. At a later stage, possibly the following year, the same students would receive follow-up training in mediation.

2.6 Justices of the Peace

The National Peace Accord and the Internal Peace Institutions Act made provision for the appointment of Justices of the Peace (JPs), their purpose being to assist Peace Committees in their duties; in other words, to give the Peace Accord teeth. The Secretariat had for some time urged Peace Committees to appoint JPs, but with little success and by April 1993 only six nominations had been received from Peace Committees. Four of these were appointed by the Minister of Justice (two for Pretoria, one for the Cape and one specifically for Wynberg), but they were not designated in terms of the Peace Institutions Act. Apparently two other persons had also been appointed (for Germiston and Johannesburg) with these functions in mind.

Negotiating Justice

In terms of the Justices of the Peace and Commissioners of Oaths Act,[52] Justices of the Peace were appointed by the Minister of Justice for as long as the Minister wished or until they were elected to a representative body, such as Parliament or a municipal council.[53] Election to public bodies involved in the negotiation process appeared to be the only statutory disqualification, but a Department of Justice brochure mentioned that, in addition, the following persons did not qualify to be appointed: practising advocates and attorneys, ministers of religion, state and municipal officials as well as officials of control boards and the National Parks Board and sheriffs. The restriction on lawyers functioning as JPs was subsequently lifted, but their functions were limited to Peace Accord work, and the same situation would possibly apply to clergy. JPs had to be between 30 and 70 years old. There were also some persons who were *ex officio* Justices of the Peace.[54]

Although all JPs were appointed in terms of the 1963 Act and had the powers as set out in the Criminal Procedure Act,[55] the Director-General of Justice could, in terms of the Internal Peace Institutions Act, designate some of them to perform particular duties and have specific powers.[56] Of these some might be required to undergo specific training. Lists of the names, addresses and telephone numbers of JPs designated in terms of the Peace Institutions Act would be kept and supplied to Peace Committees.[57]

A JP who was a member of a panel could resign from it by informing the Director-General of Justice in writing.[58] The Director-General would also be able to cancel a JP's designation to perform the duties in terms of the Internal Peace Institutions Act, but the JP would remain in office until the Minister of Justice decided otherwise. There was no limit to the number of JPs in a particular magisterial district and they performed their duties without remuneration as a community service.

It should be noted, in passing, that a South African JP is not a

---

52. Section 2.
53. See schedule 1 of Act 16 of 1963.
54. 51 of 1977.
55. Section 17(1)(a).
56. Section 17(1)(b).
57. Section 17.
58. Section 3 of Act 16 of 1963.

magistrate, as is the case in England. The South African JPs are not judicial officers and perform primarily administrative functions in an honorary capacity. South African JPs assist magistrates, who are paid civil servants and who have both judicial and administrative duties.

The ordinary powers and duties of JPs do not extend beyond the magisterial districts for which they are appointed. They must carry out any instruction by the local magistrate relating to the preservation of the peace and good order and 'render all assistance possible in suppressing disorder or disturbance in the district'.[59] In addition the Minister may at any time confer other powers or impose further duties upon a JP.[60] For example, all JPs have been designated commissioners of oaths for their magisterial districts and are regularly instructed to assist with the conduct of elections.

In addition, the Criminal Procedure Act includes JPs in its definition of 'peace officer',[61] together with magistrates and certain police and prison officials. As a result, a JP has the power to call upon a person to furnish his or her name and address, to arrest (with or without a warrant), to issue a warrant of arrest, to search a person, to enter and search premises and to seize articles and to take a confession. In all these instances, however, the JP must adhere to the procedures as set out in the Criminal Procedure Act.

The Internal Peace Institutions Act granted powers and duties to JPs as part of a package aimed at involving the community in the peace process and in settling disputes. Some JPs would be charged in future with the task of promoting peace in a particular region, but only after consultations with the relevant Regional and Local Peace Committees. Such JPs might be designated to perform their duties in areas beyond the magisterial districts for which they were originally appointed: the idea was to set up panels for each region.

While all JPs have the powers set out in the Criminal Procedure Act, only those JPs designated in terms of the Internal Peace Institutions Act would have peace-keeping functions and powers. One exception might be noted, however: if a practising attorney or advocate were to be appointed a 'peace-keeping' JP, the police-type functions had to be excluded. This, I believe, ought to have been the case for all

---

59. *Ibid.*
60. Section 1.
61. See section 18(5).

'peace-keeping' JPs. It should not have been open to them to act either in terms of the Criminal Procedure Act or the Internal Peace Institutions Act. Peace Institutions JPs should be a special breed, unassociated with the normal functions. This would have made them more acceptable to the communities, for not only would they be perceived to have an independent function, but they would not be associated with the concept of 'peace officer' into which category certain police and prison officials also fall. Peace-keeping JPs should not have had police-type powers.

At first sight it appeared that a JP's jurisdiction was limited to natural persons, not organisations or institutions. However, provided that an organisation was a juristic person, the Act would apply. A municipality's decision to cut off residents' water supply, or, as happened in Uitenhage, a municipality's decision to demand a R100,000 guarantee from organisers of protest marches to cover possible damage caused, could be adjudicated upon by a JP. On the other hand, a JP could not deal with activities of institutions without legal personality, for example, a local taxi association or community association.

How were JPs to go about their work? JPs apparently could not exercise powers in terms of the Peace Institutions Act of their own accord: they could only deal with matters which were referred to them by Peace Committees.[62] Where an LPC believed that peaceful relations in the community were being disturbed or could be disturbed by conduct which could lead to public violence and intimidation, the matter could be brought to a JP's attention. If the crimes of public violence or intimidation had already been committed JPs had no jurisdiction to consider the matter any further. However, if the JP believed that the conduct could lead to the commission of such crimes, in other words, that such conduct would disturb the peace, the JP had then to investigate the matter according to prescribed procedures set out in regulations, and where possible, attempt to resolve the matter by negotiation.[63] Most investigations would probably be held in the JP's office, although it might be necessary to conduct hearings elsewhere.

If the negotiation failed, a JP might issue a written order prohibiting

---

62. Section 18(1)(a).
63. *Ibid.*

Legislating for Peace

the particular conduct.[64] There was nothing in the Act suggesting that a JP had to be satisfied that further negotiations could not succeed, but it is suggested that such a criterion was implied in the words 'failed negotiation'. Before issuing the order, however, a JP had to take reasonable steps to hear the persons concerned.[65] Again, the purpose of this hearing was not stipulated, but since there appeared to be no reason for determining anew whether negotiations should continue, it had to be to receive representations as to the nature and type of order. It was possible to issue an order without notice to the person affected by the order, but someone who was not present when the order was issued against him or her could request that the matter be reconsidered.[66]

The procedure set out in the Act did not provide for a rehearing. Instead, a person who felt aggrieved might request the JP who made the order, or if unavailable, any other JP, to cancel the order. The JP was obliged to hear that person and might thereafter either confirm or cancel the previous order.[67] I doubt whether such procedure was fair to the aggrieved person. Not only had an order been made without notice, but the aggrieved party did not have an opportunity to hear first hand the case against him or her. Also, a JP who had already made a decision would need to be convinced, even subconsciously, that the decision should be altered. The playing field was therefore not level. The question of bias was a real one and the procedure placed an unfair burden upon the aggrieved person to convince the JP that the previous decision was incorrect. On the other hand, where another JP had to decide the issue, it was most unsatisfactory that only one party, this time the person complaining about the previous ruling, should be heard, especially in view of the fact that no record of proceedings needed to be kept. A far better procedure in such cases would have been for the matter to be heard afresh before a different JP, as was the case where, prior to an order, a JP was unable to continue with the proceedings.

A JP's order remained valid for any period determined by the JP, provided that it did not exceed three months.[68] An LPC might at any time request that JP, or if not available, any other JP, to cancel the

---

64. Section 18(2).
65. Section 18(3).
66. *Ibid.*
67. Section 18(1)(b)(ii).
68. Section 18(1)(b)(iii).

order.[69] On the other hand, an LPC might request any JP to extend the order for any further period, up to a maximum of three months, but this would only be done if the JP concerned believed that such an extension would promote peaceful relations in the community.[70]

JPs might summon or direct a person who was involved in public violence and intimidation to appear before them.[71] A summons was an order by the JP to appear before him or her at a given place and time. Like all other summonses it was served by the Sheriff of the area. A direction amounted to much the same thing, except that it was served personally by the JP. It was possible that the regulations might provide that the direction be served by a member of an LPC.

If, after an investigation, the JP believed that someone was disturbing peaceful relations, the JP might order that person to give a recognisance—an undertaking—not to disturb the peace in future.[72] This would only be done after the person had been told that such action was contemplated and after that person had had an opportunity to present his or her case. The party could be ordered to provide a guarantee of no more than R1,000, with or without sureties, to ensure that he or she adhered to the conditions of the JP's order. The maximum duration of such an order was three months, which apparently could not be extended. A JP would have to conduct another full investigation into the issue. If the conditions were not observed, the JP might declare the money forfeit to the State.[73] The person would be entitled to a hearing before a forfeiture order was made and the order had the same effect as a magistrate's civil judgment.

JPs were given extensive powers to conduct their investigations in terms of the Peace Institutions Act. They might 'at all reasonable times' enter and inspect any premises,[74] (preferably during the day, with a police officer present and with the occupants' permission—although it might not always be possible to adhere to these conditions) and question persons who might be there; and they could summon people to appear before them and require them to give evidence, answer questions, produce documents or furnish

---

69. Section 18(1)(b)(iv).
70. Section 18(4)(a).
71. *Ibid.*
72. Section 18(4)(b).
73. Section 18(10)(a).
74. Section 18(10)(b).

Legislating for Peace

information.[75] JPs also had the power to administer an oath or take an affirmation from persons before they gave evidence or answered questions. They could not arrest someone while exercising their peace-keeping duties, although they could do so in terms of the Criminal Procedure Act.

It should be noted, however, that JPs were not vested with judicial powers and as a result could not punish anyone. This was a change from the position in the Bill which was first presented to Parliament. Nonetheless, anyone who failed to comply with any order might be charged in the ordinary courts of law[76] and, if found guilty, might be liable, in the case of ignoring a summons, to a fine not exceeding R10,000 or imprisonment of up to twelve months: and for failing to adhere to an order, to a maximum fine of R20,000 or twelve months' imprisonment.

Provided that JPs acted in good faith no-one could be held liable for anything arising out of the exercise of their powers or the performance of their functions.[77] Such a provision is understandable, for if this were not the case many would have refused to serve on the panel. A little disturbing, however, bearing in mind that most JPs would not be legally trained, was the fact that the Act contains insufficient safeguards against arbitrary action by a JP. Because a JP was an administrative official, no-one had a right to appeal against the merits of the JP's order. The only safeguard lay in the common-law remedy of review on the grounds of a procedural defect or because the rules of natural justice had not been satisfied. Costly Supreme Court litigation would be one's only source for redress.

Another aspect which required some attention related to the question of protection of confidential information. This was of vital importance if the integrity of the system was to be ensured and it applied not only to JPs but also to mediators appointed by Peace Committees. The system could only work if parties were open and honest with anyone

---

75. Section 19.
76. Section 23.
77. Midgley, J.R. 'Implementing the Peace Accord: A Guide to Dispute Resolution Committees' delivered during Session 1 (Political Conflict) at the South African Association for Conflict Resolution's Fifth Annual Conference on Negotiation and Mediation in Community and Political Conflict in South Africa (25-28 November 1992).

who attempted to mediate a dispute. This required that the parties be given an assurance that any information divulged to the facilitator would be protected and that the facilitator would not be compelled to divulge such information in a court of law. Any party should have been able to claim that information given to a mediator or to a JP was privileged and that such information should not have been used as evidence without permission of the parties.

In a previous paper, delivered at the SAACI conference in November,[78] I criticised the chameleon-like role which the Act ascribed to JPs. The Act required a JP first to investigate the dispute, and if he or she came to a preliminary decision that peace could be disturbed, then to negotiate it. Thereafter, if negotiations failed, the JP could make an order relating to the matter.

The initial investigation would obviously not be conducted in an arbitrary manner, but during this stage the JP did not have to adhere to the rules of natural justice—for example, hearing the views of both parties—in forming a preliminary opinion. Once the opinion was formed the procedure reached a second stage. In this context 'negotiate' was an unfortunate term, for it implied that a JP must enter the fray and persuade parties to behave differently. Apparently the term was not in the original draft legislation, but was inserted in order to conform with the wording of chapter 7 of the Peace Accord. It is therefore necessary to consider its procedural effect. The term implies a limitation on the type of action that a JP could take: mediation was excluded. However, in these kinds of cases 'mediation' was often the most appropriate dispute resolution method. The JP could then act as an independent facilitator and aim to help parties to achieve a settlement between themselves. In practice JPs would probably mediate, thus stretching the term 'negotiation' beyond its accepted meaning. The criticism of the term is not a mere semantic or academic quibble. Mediation and negotiation, although related, are entirely different concepts and the statute should have recognised that fact. Perhaps it was because mediators had been scantily used at a national political level—CODESA was a negotiating forum—that the drafters of the Peace Accord and of the legislation failed to emphasise the

---

78. Hansard 16 June 1992 col. 11324.

Legislating for Peace

difference. It was to be hoped that Parliament would rectify this error; but if it did not, JPs were likely to strain the meaning of the concept 'negotiation' and mediate disputes where necessary.

However, the JP's position was complicated even further when the Act ascribed to the person a third role by granting him or her the power to issue an order if the negotiations failed. For the JP now to make an order deciding the dispute one way or another, having been a party to the negotiation, would be a clear violation of the basic tenet of natural justice, that no decision-maker should be party to the cause which is to be decided upon. This was a ground for review by the Supreme Court, but even if it can be argued that the Act provided for such a situation to obtain, such a provision was not only morally wrong, but legally bad.

There were two possible interpretations as to the nature of the proceedings set out in the Act. The first is that the JP was now involved in a variation of what is commonly referred to as 'medarb', a dispute resolution method whereby a person first attempts to mediate an issue and if unsuccessful then resorts to deciding the merits of the dispute. The procedure has been subject to almost universal criticism, for the independent third party is confronted with two roles which not only have different functions, but also impose conflicting ethical pressures upon the third party. A mediator does not decide issues, an arbitrator does. A mediator often encourages parties to make confidential disclosures to the mediator so as to understand the interests involved. Where it is known that the third party may eventually arbitrate the dispute, parties may decide not to disclose potentially adverse information during the mediation process. This places a handicap on the process. On the other hand, where confidential information is disclosed to the mediator it is unlikely that this will be ignored when the process is converted to that of arbitration. No matter how hard one tries, the danger remains that the information will have a subconscious influence.

The second interpretation is that the Act did not at all envisage a 'medarb' situation, but that the JP remained an arbitrator who, as all good arbitrators should, was enjoined to promote settlement of an issue throughout the proceedings. JPs were not mediators, and the Act did not allow JPs to don such mantles. The net effect is that JPs would follow procedures more akin to those in courts. While JPs remained at all times adjudicators, the Act constrained them to promote voluntary

Negotiating Justice

settlements of the issues by the parties—a form of self-discipline—thus eliminating the need to make orders. But JPs had to act within the context of the adjudication process, in the same way as judicial officers.

Although the second interpretation would eliminate the conflicts mentioned above, I remain convinced that the Act did more than create a judicial officer-type role for JPs. I am still of the opinion that a 'medarb' situation would result in practice, and I believe that the Act should have been amended in order to clarify JPs' roles. Since JPs would be approached only when Peace Committees had been unable to deal with issues, and since a mediation function was vested in the Peace Committees, there should have been no ambiguity concerning JPs' arbitration functions. This was in fact what was required to give the process teeth. One then eliminated the danger that JPs might enter the fray as parties to issues, for example, by acting as a public official against someone instead of acting as an independent person.

Some concern had also been expressed at the fact that JPs would not be remunerated. The office was likely to be a strenuous and time-consuming one and the question of paying JPs an honorarium should have been considered.

Another fundamental issue was that of independence. Would the JP be sufficiently independent not to be influenced by role players in the community? This issue was apparently one of the reasons for the reluctance of Peace Committees to put forward names for nomination. A possible safeguard would have been to insist that two JPs be appointed to deal with a particular issue, with some mechanism to deal with possible deadlocks between them. This would also have addressed another problem area which had been identified, namely, that JPs might place themselves in danger when unpopular decisions were made. Joint responsibility might have gone some way to diffuse the situation. But there might have been financial constraints and, as has been suggested, the possibility of endangering two lives.

Independence has another aspect to it. One of the concerns in the debate surrounding JPs was whether or not LPCs would be able to retain their independence in the eyes of the community, especially where a JP had made an unpopular, although necessary, order. Given the nature and the powers of the office, a JP was likely to be seen as an extension of the system for the administration of justice. LPCs are not viewed in this way. If LPC members were too closely associated with the office of a JP, for example in that they had the power to serve a JP's direction, even if it was not used, a link between the LPC and the administration of justice was established. The credibility of the entire system would then be put to the test. It was essential, even though JPs and LPCs must have a good working relationship, that they were not too closely associated.

Communities were reluctant to submit names of possible JPs to the Secretariat. The question was, 'Why?' The Secretariat pointed to the fact that it was difficult to find suitable candidates—individuals who could rise above the fray. Past allegiances seemed to be a major issue, but another concern was to find unaligned persons who could deal with issues fairly and independently. Apparently, in a number of cases when names had been put before LPCs the impartiality of the nominees was questioned, often only in an attempt to ensure that politically sympathetic people were appointed. Lawyers may have been trained to fulfil this role, but since this work fell squarely within their professional sphere, one could not expect them to offer such services on a voluntary basis.

There were also other issues which caused concern. Many had doubts about the viability of the system which was a Western-style concept and, according to some, a mere extension of an already unacceptable system. Other possibilities were the danger involved in performing JP duties in some areas, the lack of remuneration, the lack of clarity concerning the role of JPs within the peace structures, the lack of proper marketing, and the lack of consultation at local levels.

I believe that another reason for the apathy was lack of information. It was not enough to say to grassroots structures that the Peace Accord made provision for JPs and that therefore they should put forward names. Or, even worse, 'We haven't set out exactly what a peace-keeping JP's powers will be, or what procedures JPs will follow, but trust us to do the right thing.' Peace Committees wished to be informed of, and understand, the structures which they were expected to endorse. They were not prepared to sign a blank cheque on scant information. The structure was unlikely to be supported, I think, without proper marketing and extensive consultation.

2.7 The Management Model

The Deputy Minister of Justice at the time pointed out in Parliament that the structures were designed according to a management model whereby the initiatives and responsibility to establish peace at grassroots level rested with groups and their leaders at local and regional levels.[79] Similar sentiments were liberally scattered throughout the Peace Accord; for example, in chapter 7 it was stated that RPCs and LPCs were to gain their legitimacy by representing the people and the communities they were designed to serve. The Internal Peace Institutions Act itself mentioned that RPCs and LPCs were to combat violence and intimidation as representatives of the community.[80]

The above-mentioned sentiments pointed to the fact that we should have been dealing with a structure whereby communities assumed responsibility for establishing peace, and in my experience this was happening in practice. The sentiments also implied a bottom-up model, in which a committee is accountable to its community for its actions. It is interesting to note, however, that neither the Peace Accord nor the Act made provision for LPC representation on regional committees, nor for RPC representation on the national structure. Grassroots accountability, it seemed, was to be achieved indirectly through particular organisations' regional structures, even where such organisations did not operate in a community in which an LPC was active. Such a model also did not recognise the inadequate channels of communication that currently existed in organisations and political parties. Individual RPCs might have realised and responded to this problem and might have provided for LPC representation, but it should have been redressed everywhere.

A disturbing feature of the Act's passage through Parliament was the unilateral way in which the legislation was implemented. We were informed that there had been some input from individuals in COSATU and the IFP, but the procedures which had been agreed upon were not followed. Therefore the commitment of the parliamentary parties to the provisions of the Peace Accord was dented, for they ignored the fact that they had agreed in that document that '[i]n drafting the required legislation there should be wide consultation including with the

---

79. See the italicised portion of the section quoted in the text above.
80. Clause 7.14.

Legislating for Peace

National Peace Committee' and that the 'proposed legislation will also be published for general information and comment'.[81] These terms of the social contract were as important as those concerning the conduct of police and political parties, if not more so, for they struck to the root of the legitimacy of the statutory structures. If government cared to ignore these terms, what guarantee did the public have that it would honour others which it considered to be inexpedient? The Government therefore could not object to the possible scepticism with which the Act was viewed, for its actions invited this. There seemed to be no good reason for the inordinate haste with which the legislation was passed. The administrative difficulties, such as finances, could have been addressed in another way. The structures were already in place and for almost ten months after being passed the Act's nuts and bolts, the regulations, did not see the light of day. The statutory structure, too, was not implemented immediately, so urgency could not have been a valid reason for rushing through the legislation. By 1993 the Government still appeared not to have realised fully the implications of President De Klerk's commitment to negotiation politics: that process is often more important than outcome.

Closer analysis of the *de facto* management model reveals that it bore very little resemblance to the sentiments and principles enunciated above. In practice the model had a definite top-down structure which showed little deviation from that of traditional hierarchical corporate management. The Directorate was the equivalent to a company's head office, and the RPCs and LPCs were its branches. The consumers, the community, or the voluntary workforce, were not catered for in the structure. Statements and conduct of members of the Secretariat confirmed this attitude. In one of its reports the Secretariat stated that political leaders had insufficient discipline over party members who continued to conduct political activities at Peace Committee level instead of working together in implementing the Peace Accord. However, this was part of the political processes at work in South African society. The person at local level wished to participate in the political process and would not accept and obey commands from leaders without proper consultation. Similarly, the Secretariat showed remarkable insensitivity in its marketing of Justices of the Peace. We had been told that it would continue with the designation and training

---

81. Above, n. *23*.

of the four nominees, despite the concerns expressed by Peace Committees throughout the country. The impression was that the Secretariat did not see itself in a partnership with communities in the peace process. Communities had been given the duty to manage peace but their input was ignored.

The system's structure appeared to be at the heart of the problem. At grassroots level people were likely to feel betrayed, for many local organisations had been drawn into the process on the strength of what they had read in the Peace Accord and by the fact that their national structures had signed the Accord. Now they found that in theory at least, if not in practice, they were accountable, through the committees, to the Minister of Justice and the State President. The hurt in our society could not be wished away overnight and the following comments by Lamola should therefore not come as a surprise:[82]

> The very same political parties which are calling for an independent multiparty structure to command the security forces in their dealings with violence, have allowed the minority National Party Government to have a supreme responsibility in the organisation and servicing of the instruments of institutions of internal peace.

And

> The [Act] provides for the headship of the National Peace Secretariat by an Executive Director who is appointed by the Minister of Justice 'subject to the laws governing the Public Service'. The very same Minister of Justice is at the same time responsible for the National Intelligence Service which is still being used to keep tabs on the opponents of the National Party.

There was a very real perception in some quarters that in winning the hearts and minds of the communities, the legislation had created mechanisms whereby communities would also become the eyes and

---

82. Cleary, S. 'Democratic Values as a Normative Reference Point: A Track Two Approach to Conflict Resolution in South Africa' delivered during Session 1 (Political Conflict) at the South African Association for Conflict Resolution's Fifth Annual Conference on Negotiation and Mediation in Community and Political Conflict in South Africa (25-28 November 1992).

Legislating for Peace

ears of the security forces. In short, the fear was that the Act extended the old management committee system and would create a nation of informers.

Some may feel that my analysis of the situation is unduly harsh, for in establishing LPCs people were at pains to follow an inclusive approach in order to get the support of as many organisations and institutions as possible. They will point to the standing of LPCs in various communities and to the successes that had been achieved, and remind one that LPCs had regular plenary meetings at which report-backs were made and at which input could be received. If the structures were not acceptable, they would not have been used.

These points are valid. Nonetheless, members of peace structures should have been sensitive to the organisational difficulties which the system faces. One cannot just point to the Peace Accord's heritage, and the process through which it was established, proclaim them to have been good and acceptable, and rely on the past when structures face new challenges. When LPCs were established, communities were interested in being able to participate in regulating their affairs, to taste aspects of democracy. They were hopeful and expectant; some were suspicious, but daring enough to give the concept a try. Others were constrained to participate, despite more deep-rooted suspicion, by the fact that various national structures had signed the Peace Accord. The first few months were fascinating for many. Communities were discovering themselves. But that 'honeymoon' would disappear and, to mix metaphors, the structures would undergo a period of adolescence. For some this process had already begun.

It would have been surprising if, in reality, more than a handful of LPCs, within a year of their establishment in July 1992, still adhered to the principles of a community-based management model. The reasons are as follows. First, although some LPCs arose out of community initiatives (and even where they did not), such LPCs were immediately drawn into a national structure and made subject to the direction and control of committees and government departments which had little or no accountability to the grassroots structures. These committees and departments were responsible to the Secretariat and ultimately to the State President, the Minister of Justice and to Parliament. Secondly, most Peace Committees were headed by business people or clergy. In fact, LPCs were encouraged to draw their chairpersons from these sectors of society. Without casting any doubt upon their efficiency, integrity or acumen, the fact remained that both categories of people were familiar with the traditional hierarchical way of running institutions. The emphasis was bound to be on streamlining decision-making, on avoiding the waste of time, on efficiency, results and getting things done—Western-style values—instead of concentrating on the legitimacy of the structure, on incorporating ordinary people into the decision-making process and on having regular and effective consultation and report-backs so that everyone was kept informed and up to date. Executive committees would be formed which would make all the important decisions, as a matter of efficient administration, but at the risk of alienating those who were interested in participating in the peace process. I believe that many LPCs would be either oblivious to the risk, or would simply ignore the need for a change of style. As a result, there was a real danger that LPCs would become marginalised by the community. Practices of the workplace had been introduced into the community arena, but the controls which existed in business did not exist there.

My plea, therefore, was that the Secretariat and the Peace Committees should recognise that they existed to build peace in our communities and that they should concentrate on establishing and maintaining relationships in an attempt to achieve this objective. To do so, would mean a return to the management model originally envisaged in the Peace Accord.

3 CONCLUSION

This paper tries to give more than just an overview of the nature and activities of the Peace Accord structures. In doing so it may have sketched a scenario of despondency, but I hope not. South Africa is unique in its attempt to address violence by legislating for peace. The Peace Accord's value lies in the fact that it contains a set of values for society. It is an exciting thought that structures can be created through which a greatly divided society can become actively involved in civic affairs, in partnership with opponents and long-standing enemies. As Cleary said at the SAACI conference in November 1992, 'the process demonstrated that South Africans from a wide range of political

Legislating for Peace

persuasions were able to rise above sectional interests and cooperate....'[83] In effect, we have created a Ministry of Peace to assist healing the wounds in our society and to promote an ethos of tolerance for others which is so lacking.

There were many who were sceptical about the Peace Accord's efficacy. Some pointed to the excessive violence which was racking the country and to the increase in violence and killings since the Accord was drafted. Others noted that Peace Committees became forums for political expression and power play. One could not deny these realities, but it was simplistic merely to point fingers at the Peace Accord. Unfortunately, Cleary was also correct in pointing out that the Accord defined the key elements of a future political culture, but not the current one, and that the Accord's failure had been due largely to the parties' failure to honour their obligations. Pieces of paper are not always enough: enormous effort is also required to ensure that the values decided upon at the negotiating table are also accepted by the ordinary members of society. Nossel and Sher pointed out at the same conference[84] that South Africans were working within a paradigm of peace-making, peace-keeping and peace-building. The first function had been assumed by political leaders, whether through multiparty or bilateral talks, whether at CODESA[85] or elsewhere. They mention that it is 'the formal process of negotiation used to transform a situation of conflict into óne in which peaceful coexistence is possible'. The second concerned issues of law and order, and fell within the tasks of the police and other security forces. The purpose of this function was not to address the causes of violence, but to control the manifestations of conflict. As regards peace-building, Nossel and Sher point out:[86]

> Peacebuilding functions are aimed at the transformation of
> societal conditions and attitudes which surround conflict.

---

83. Sher M. and Nossel S. 'Groundswell at the Grassroots: The Challenge Posed by Peace Accord Dispute Resolution Committees' delivered during Session 1 (Political Conflict) at the South African Association for Conflict Resolution's Fifth Annual Conference on Negotiation and Mediation in Community and Political Conflict in South Africa (25-28 November 1992).
84. The Convention For a Democratic South Africa was a multi-party negotiating forum consisting of nineteen delegations. It met for the first time in December 1991. It has since been reconstituted.
85. Above, n. 83.
86. Above, n. 83.

> Peacebuilding initiatives work to reverse the mindsets of hostility and adversarialism which are entrenched in societies plagued by sustained conflict. Peacebuilding efforts seek to ensure that shifts which occur as a result of agreements at leadership level are accompanied by corresponding movement in *inter*-party views and perceptions at grassroots. Peacebuilding structures in contemporary South Africa include all initiatives underway to bridge political and racial divisions at community level.

Peace-building was the Accord's purpose: relationship-building and engaging people at grassroots level. If the Peace Accord is measured against its role in the paradigm, then one sees a different picture. People defined and developed interests across political and racial divides; individuals and communities became empowered, for there was now increased access to decision-making structures and an increase in problem-solving skills. People in the street, in defiance of what was happening at national level, had a capacity for delivering results on local issues, and used this capacity. It was often said that participation in Peace Committees allowed for interaction with opponents without anyone losing political credibility. The peace process introduced multiparty engagement and political accountability at a local level, and was preparing societies for a democracy.

The Peace Accord was therefore a document which promised a peaceful future, for it emphasised common vision and set out proper standards of community interaction. The daunting aspect was that we could not afford to see it fail.

Chapter Seven

Conclusion

Malyn Newitt and Mervyn Bennun

This is a book about South Africa between 1990 and 1994, about the first stage of decolonisation and the making of the first democratic constitution. This final section reviews briefly the power struggles, legal arguments and ideological debates which culminated in the elections of April 1994 and the swearing in of President Mandela; and at the programmes being developed for the future.

1 THE PROCESS OF TRANSITION

During July 1993 a dramatic shift of political alliances took place. President F.W. De Klerk's Government moved from virtually open support for Inkatha and the idea of a quasi-federal constitution to an equally emphatic alliance with the ANC. It was a political shift with its own inner dynamics; in a letter a few months earlier to Nelson Mandela[1] he had complained that the South African Communist Party 'played a dominant role in redirecting the ANC from negotiations to the politics of demands and confrontation which are inherent in mass mobilisation'. On 16 July 1992 the South African Minister of Foreign Affairs, 'Pik' Botha, addressed the United Nations' Security Council and demanded to know of the ANC whether it had shed the doctrines which, he claimed, the SACP insisted should be included in the new constitution; and whether the ANC would reveal the names of SACP

---

1. Dated 9 July 1992, and released by the ANC; part of an exchange of correspondence between President F.W. De Klerk and Nelson Mandela.

members on its executive. De Klerk demanded that the ANC should resume the negotiations it had broken off following the Boipatong massacre;[2] this had been the final straw so far as the ANC was concerned, as the organisation had repeatedly claimed that the State was at the least derelict in its duty to investigate and prevent violence, and at worst responsible for causing it. In any event, the ANC ignored the attacks on its links with the Communist Party, although there was intense debate[3] within the two organisations about the relationship between them as two members of what became known as the 'Triple Alliance'—the African National Congress, the SACP, and the Congress of South African Trades Unions (COSATU). By mid-August, however, the press was noting 'Mandela's positive words about De Klerk',[4] though in October De Klerk still said that he would not form an interim government with the African National Congress until it had 'got rid of the radicals'.[5]

It was also a shift which brought quick results. Agreement was reached on a Transitional Executive Council (TEC) in September 1992 and on 18 November 1992 the final details of an interim constitution were completed. When the elections took place in April 1994 many commentators spoke as though this ANC-National Party alliance had existed unbroken since 1990 and was the inevitable result of far-seeing and generous statesmanship by Mandela and De Klerk.[6]

This idea of the 'magnanimous gesture' in which acts of political courage and daring bring reconciliation to erstwhile opponents is part of the mythology of South African history. It played its part in bringing English and Afrikaner communities together after the Boer War and such political myths may always be essential if different communities are to forget their past hostilities and live together. Certainly the events

---

2. Statement of the Emergency Meeting of the National Executive Committee of the ANC, 23 June, 1992; African National Congress Department of Information and Publicity (Johannesburg).
3. See, for example, 'Interview with Allan Boesak: Is he Anti-Communist?' (1991, Third Quarter) *African Comunist* 6; and the letter in reply thereto by Blade Nzimande; (1991, Fourth Quarter) *African Communist* 46. Dr Boesak had just been elected to the Chair of the ANC's Western Cape branch.
4. *Independent*, 11 August 1992.
5. *Morning Star*, 14 October 1992.
6. 'A Two Saint Miracle', *The Times* 27 April 1994.

Conclusion

of April were to be rich in the symbolic, 'myth-making', acts of peace and unity.

However, as this book has shown, the politics of the period after 1990 do not conform very closely to this mythical image of peace and cooperation. From 1990 the National Party certainly pursued a policy of trying to destabilise the ANC, initially with the hope of forging a widespread anti-ANC coalition designed to pivot on Inkatha as a dominant black organisation. During the referendum campaign of March 1992, in which the white electorate was asked if it wished the government to continue the process of negotiating a new constitution, Inkatha had urged whites to vote 'yes' to achieve 'the establishment of one sovereign parliament opposite to the CP model which wants the country to be broken up into national states'.[7] In the light of the stance that Inkatha subsequently took, such a declaration only becomes comprehensible when it is understood that at that time Inkatha and the De Klerk Government were working in close alliance and even envisaged the victory of an anti-ANC coalition.

An important instrument for the destabilisation of the ANC were units of the SADF, notably the Directorate of Military Intelligence (DMI). Towards the end of March 1994 the Goldstone Commission received detailed inside information about these activities from senior officers, and the full extent of the involvement of the police and army in the murder campaigns was revealed.[8] The result of this policy was certainly to fuel the township violence, while at the same time the NP was successful in winning support from the coloured and Indian communities and preventing widespread defections by whites to the extreme right-wing organisations.

However, by the end of 1992 the destabilisation of the ANC was rapidly becoming the destabilisation of South Africa as a whole, and De Klerk moved for the first time against dissident elements in the security forces that had clearly been operating not only outside public accountability but outside control of the Government itself. The

---

7. Annette Strauss, 'The 1992 Referendum in South Africa', (1993, 2, xxxi) *Journal of Modern African Studies*, pp. 339-360, p. 348.
8. 'Police Informers led Goldstone to rightwing terror network', *Guardian*, 19 March 1994; John Carlin, 'De Klerk's blind eye to slaughter', *Independent* 20 March 1994; see also Herbert M.Howe, 'The South African Defence Force and Political Reform', (1994, 1, xxxii) *Journal of Modern African Studies*, pp.29-51.

Negotiating Justice

political calculation made by De Klerk and his advisers was that, with the troubled state of the country and with the capacity of the right-wing forces to destabilise it having been demonstrated, a power sharing deal with the ANC was a more realistic possibility than a victory for an anti-ANC coalition. The ANC had, indeed, been softened up enough for important constitutional concessions to be won. However, there was another important consideration. In spite of the encouragement which western governments had given to the white electorate at the time of the 1992 referendum, international sanctions had not been lifted and investment had not begun to flow into the country again. The business community, representing the interests of influential parts of the white community, wanted more rapid progress.

It was a strategy that was full of risks, for De Klerk would have to face the rage of the betrayed white right wing and the resentment of Buthelezi and the other Homeland leaders. The political logic, however, was inexorable. The NP had originally been founded as the party of the poor white Afrikaner. Steadily the basis for its support had shifted. In the 1950s and 1960s it was widely backed by educated, middle class Afrikaners and was the party of the massive apartheid bureaucracy and security forces. The 1970s and 1980s saw the Afrikaner working class largely dropped and the English whites brought into the NP fold. The quarrels over the 1983 constitution saw the Afrikaner civil servants and security personnel desert to the Conservative Party (CP) so that Botha found himself dependent now on the votes of English (and Portuguese) speaking whites for his continued majority. After 1990 the National Party sought to take on board a new constituency of coloureds, Indians and dissident African bourgeoisie. How could this be done without a major backlash from whites long accustomed to supremacy? As Simon Jenkins was to write in *The Times*,[9]

> The Cabinet had to move fast and yet reassure its supporters that De Klerk's grip was sure. The whites had to be in control even of the process of losing control.

The calculation that the NP cabinet had made was that, even if earlier hopes of formal power sharing, a white veto, or a white

---

9. Simon Jenkins, 'A Two Saint Miracle', *The Times* 27 April 1994.

Conclusion

dominated federation would have to be abandoned, the ANC could be pressured into making sufficient concessions to make the transfer of power a gradual process. The NP cabinet hoped that this gradual process that would not endanger property and would leave the socio-economic structures of white power in place even if whites had to abandon formal political control.

That the alliance with the ANC was a political calculation rather than a genuine conversion to social justice and multi-racial ideals emerged during the April election campaign when National Party election literature openly and unequivocally turned to racial themes in seeking the votes of the coloureds of the Cape. The theme of the *swart gevaar* ('black menace') was allowed to dominate the campaign in 1994 just as it had in 1948.

The link with the ANC rapidly bore fruit as a series of compromise deals were worked out in the CODESA constitutional forum. In July 1993 the draft of the interim constitution was tabled, the signal for Buthelezi and the CP to withdraw from negotiations.[10] Early in September the Transitional Executive was established with the task of 'promoting conditions conducive to the holding of free and fair elections'.[11] On September 24th international sanctions against South Africa were formally lifted, and the final agreements on a transitional constitution were reached on November 18th.

The transitional constitution established a 400 person National Assembly, half of whose members would represent regions and half be selected from party lists. There would be a 90 seat Senate as an upper house. The cabinet was to be made up proportionately from all parties gaining 5 per cent of the vote and decisions in the cabinet were to be by 'consensus, in a manner which gives consideration to the spirit underlying the concept of a government of national unity'. The new Assembly was charged with drawing up a permanent constitution based on certain established principles and the Government was to remain until elections that would be held in 1999. The essence of this transitional constitution was that, although it did not allow for a white veto, or for a formalised power-sharing arrangement (for which De Klerk had clearly at one time been pressing and which he had made all

---

10. 'South Africa's unholy alliance hints at war', *Observer* 25 July 1993.
11. 'Interim body to steer S.Africa to election', *Guardian* 2 September 1993.

along the central plank of his appeal to white voters) it did provide for a five year transition period in which, in effect, South Africa would be ruled by a government in which whites would hold key ministries. Moreover the constitution made provision for a Bill of Rights and set up an independent Constitutional Court to enforce it. The future might not hold a vision of power-sharing or of a federal constitution but it presented a very different prospect from the sort of transfer of power which had taken place in other parts of Africa.

Marginalised by these moves, Buthelezi, some of the Homeland leaders and the forces of the Afrikaner extreme right, temporarily united by general Constand Viljoen in the Volksfront, had absented themselves in July 1993 from the constitutional process and had therefore played no role in the final drafting processes. Instead they had formed the Freedom Alliance, with the avowed intention of preventing the election taking place, and of forcing an extreme form of federalism on the country. Although many commentators saw this as a potentially formidable alliance, capable of sabotaging the election and of carrying the country into civil war, its political effectiveness collapsed in early 1994.

The Freedom Alliance disintegrated for a variety of reasons but at the root of its failure were fundamental problems with the concept of federalism. Although a federation based loosely on the old Homelands was at least a structure that could be said to have existed after a fashion under the old constitution, nobody imagined that the 85 per cent of white-controlled South Africa could remain as the white-dominated part of the federation. So where could an Afrikaner or a white Homeland be found?

The ANC stated publicly that it was prepared to discuss the issue of a white Homeland and as late as 31 January 1994 there were still formal talks between De Klerk, Mandela, and the leaders of the white right-wing about the prospects of such a *Volkstaat*.[12]

In retrospect this can be seen as supremely artful politics. Far from selling the birthright of Africans on the very eve of their independence, these 'negotiations' over a white Homeland proved to be a policy for dividing Afrikaners—for preventing the old ox-wagon becoming in effect a bandwagon. Should the white Homeland be in the Northern Cape? What better way to alienate the Afrikaners of the Transvaal and

---

12. 'Mandela promises not to nationalise white farms', *Guardian* 1 February 1994.

Conclusion

OFS. Should it be located somewhere in the old trekker republics? But where could a large enough white-controlled area of land be found? And what about a way to the sea? There are echoes here of the politics of the late nineteenth century. By mid-1993 the extreme right was floundering in a disorganised muddle of maps, each one producing a more and more bizarre formulation of the Volkstaat.[13]

This fundamental disagreement soon resulted in a deep disagreement over tactics, as one faction sought to fight the elections and another to take up armed insurrection. General Viljoen led one group, called the Freedom Front, to fight the elections and they eventually won 2.2 per cent of the vote. Armed insurrection, on the other hand, soon became a grim farce as trigger-happy AWB supporters rode into Bophutatswana on 13 March 1994 to support the Homeland Government of President Mangope. The dispersal of this invading force by the black security forces and the summary execution of two white gunmen in front of television cameras had a dramatic and symbolic impact—'the definitive image of a generations-old battle finally lost', as David Cohen of the *Independent* wrote on 30 March; a cold and controlled act of finality which contrasted so vividly with the chaos, cruelty and blindness of the township violence.[14] By July 1994 *Jane's Intelligence Review* concluded that Eugene Terre'Blanche, the AWB's leader, had 'failed dismally' and he and his organisation were generally written off.[15]

An important aspect of the failure of the fringe right-wing groups was the lack of support for a coup from the SADF and the police. Until the end of 1992 De Klerk had not moved against the South African military establishment and the destabilisation policies were being carried forward, apparently with government connivance. It has been pointed out that in acting in this way De Klerk was very much in the tradition of P.W. Botha who had always sought to strengthen his power base within the white electorate by unleashing the SADF against soft

---

13. B.M. du Toit, 'The Far Right in Current South African Politics', (1991 29, iv) *Journal of Modern South African Politics*, pp.627-667.
14. David Cohen, 'Alwyn's Last Trek', *Independent* 30 March 1994.
15. 'British Experts write off ET's men', *Weekly Mail and Guardian*, July 15-21, 1994. On the same page another report, 'Just a pile of empty bottles where the AWB waited for war', describes a AWB camp abandoned as Terre'Blanche and his disillusioned members lost heart.

black targets in the frontline states. However the military budget had steadily been reduced since 1990 and the manpower of the SADF cut back.[16] De Klerk calculated that the loyalty of the SADF could be maintained while its capacity to stage a coup was being weakened, if it was still left very much to run itself and was not called to account for past crimes. Moreover there were obvious advantages in keeping highly trained military personnel in the armed forces and under military discipline, in preference to demobilising them and providing them as recruits for the right-wing para-militaries.

Within the armed forces and the police, personal calculations were being made. On the one hand there were the formidable risks of a coup; on the other, the risks—different but equally great—of entering a new order with the doings of the past unexpunged. In the last days of March the Goldstone Commission was inundated with army and police officers hastening to give evidence of destabilising activities in the hope of putting themselves on a good footing with the new regime. There could be no surer sign of the collapse of any resolve within the security forces to continue the war against the ANC, than this opening of the sluices of information.[17]

Meanwhile, the Homeland governments themselves had collapsed as a basis for support for federalism and the Freedom Alliance. Observers of the Homelands over a number of years had seen the erosion of the power base of the Homeland leaders as they failed to win support from the black middle classes.[18] Political power had rested increasingly on the armed forces and police, and on a bureaucracy more or less closely linked with Pretoria. Inkatha apart, ethnically-based populist movements, although tried, never rivalled the ANC as a focus for mass political aspirations. The march back into South Africa was led by Venda and the Transkei, two of the four Homelands that had been made technically independent by Pretoria. The reward for Holomisa (Transkei) and Ramushwana (Venda) was to achieve a place on the ANC's list of candidates for Parliament.[19] With a shift of power

---

16. Herbert M.Howe, 'The South African Defence Force and Political Reform', (1994, 1, xxxii) *Journal of Modern African Studies*, pp.29-51.
17. 'Goldstone informers "hidden" abroad', *Guardian* 25 March 1993.
18. Leslie Bank, 'Between traders and tribalists: implosion and the politics of disjuncture in a South Africa homeland', (1994, 370, xciii) *African Affairs*, pp.75-98.
19. 'Mandela on course for poll triumph', *Observer* 16 January 1994.

Conclusion

imminent, significant groups in the other Homelands abandoned the idea of federalism and threw in their lot with the perceived inheritors of power, the ANC. A mutiny in Bophutatswana provided the opportunity for De Klerk's Government to dethrone Lucas Mangope and bring Bophutatswana into the electoral process, and in the dying days of March the Transitional Executive installed new administrations in Ciskei, Qwa Qwa and Lebowa.

There remained Inkatha. Inkatha at least had a high profile leadership, a populist ideology that certainly attracted a significant element of popular support, and a bureaucratic and military base. Throughout 1993 Buthelezi had scarcely disguised his ambition of seeking a Zulu state which would be independent or quasi-independent. Against his political opponents he increasingly put on parade the Zulu king as a focus for national unity and as a symbol of the viability of the new state. But throughout 1993 opinion polls showed a relentless decline in support and in January 1994 they showed Inkatha with barely 5 per cent of the vote nationally and only 25 per cent in kwaZulu-Natal.[20] Discount their accuracy as he might, the impression spread that Buthelezi was leader, not of a viable party, but of an increasingly marginalised fraction which could not even command majority support in kwaZulu let alone among Zulu speakers in the country as a whole.

Inkatha faced an acute problem in, on the one hand, trying to pose as a national party capable of replacing the NP as the main opposition to the ANC, while at the same time claiming to represent the Zulus and playing for what was in substance a Zulu national state. However, there were other reasons for Buthelezi's failure. Increasingly Inkatha and the kwaZulu police were perceived to be responsible for the violence in the townships and the rural areas of Natal.[21] As late as the summer of 1993 Inkatha shared this reputation with the security forces, but De Klerk's avowed shift of political stance was increasingly successful in distancing the Government from the violence. The declaration of a state of emergency in Natal on 31 March 1994, ineffective as it proved to be, put a final coat of whitewash on the

---

20. *Ibid.*; and see Simon Jenkins, n. 6, above.
21. For a review of some aspects and incidents, see the Third Interim Report of the Goldstone Commission (Commission of enquiry regarding the prevention of public violence and intimidation); Judge Richard Goldstone (chair); Cape Town, 6 December 1993.

reputation of the Government. Inkatha was left, in the public eye and certainly in the eye of the world, as the principal perpetrator of violence and mayhem. The state of emergency cannot have been unrelated to the work of the Goldstone Commission, which published an interim report on 18 March 1994 setting out evidence it had obtained on allegations against the South African and kwaZulu Police, and the Inkatha Freedom Party.[22] This report is little less than astounding; if substantiated, there is overwhelming confirmation of the allegations that high-ranking members of these bodies had abused their positions and had committed crimes such as murder, the organisation of 'hit squads', and the supply of illegal arms, and had taken steps to cover and conceal their activities. It is highly significant how the Commission explained its decision to publish the information it held:[23]

> The Commission would have liked to have had additional time in order to investigate more thoroughly a myriad of allegations made by many witnesses. However, with the election now less than 6 weeks away the members of the Commission and its counsel came to the unanimous decision that with the corroboration already at hand it has no option but to bring all the information contained in this report to the attention of the public. If those intent on further destabilisation succeed in aborting the election an investigation afterwards would be a futile exercise.

The defeat of the Freedom Alliance was nevertheless a complex and sophisticated political operation. There was certainly an international dimension, as Britain and the United States made it clear that breakaway groups would not gain any international recognition. Significant also was the fact that the newspapers were full of the catastrophe of Angola, where ethnically-based political strongmen had brought chaos and horror to a country where international observers had decreed elections to have been free and fair.

Angola was no end of a lesson. One of Africa's richest countries had been brought to a state of ruin in which white property owners and

---

22. Goldstone Commission (Commission of inquiry regarding the prevention of public violence and intimidation), 'Interim report on criminal political violence by elements within the South African Police, the kwaZulu Police, and the Inkatha Freedom Party; 18 March 1994.
23. Above, n. 22, para. 23.1.

Conclusion

the middle classes had been among the principal victims. Moreover it was a country in which foreign intervention had become a matter of routine—not the relatively rational intervention of governments with coherent agendas, but the intervention of gangsters, adventurers, religious fanatics and unemployed Cold War warriors. Could the same thing happen in South Africa? Was it perhaps already happening? Stories of RENAMO support for Inkatha, if technically unproven, seemed too credible to be ignored. Moreover most commentators agreed that it had been a mistake in the case of Angola for an election to be held on a winner-take-all basis. It created an understandable feeling among minority groups that fighting elections was not worthwhile. Elections would merely entrench the power of existing élites and bring no benefits at all to others.

It was almost certainly such considerations that underlay the astonishing political moves of early April.

With only a week to the start of polling, with international mediation having failed, and with Inkatha still opposing the whole electoral process, the Zulu king was persuaded to withdraw his backing for Inkatha's boycott.[24] Such a dramatic move was bought at a price. Publicly the king was promised the status of a constitutional monarch over the former Zulu kingdom but it also seems that behind the scenes there was a significant land deal with large areas of Zulu land transferred to a Trust under the king's control. The control of three million hectares of kwaZulu/Natal[25]—a third of the former Bantustan—was ceded to King Zwelethini by De Klerk at the very end of his Presidency.[26] The significance of this transfer is not yet fully clear: for example, it may mean that future governments in kwaZulu/Natal will have to gain the permission of the king before the land can be developed. However, it was part of a strategy which on the one hand successfully divided the king from Buthelezi and on the other made this land less accessible to the policies of the central government.

A thwarted Buthelezi, barely able to disguise his sense of defeat to the world's media, was forced to take part in the election.[27] It was to

---

24. 'Mandela takes vote to Zulu heartland', *Observer* 17 April 1994.
25. As part of the deal with Buthelezi referred to below, the territory was renamed thus.
26. 'Land deal: the king's ransom', *Weekly Mail and Guardian* 20-26 May 1994.
27. For an account of the events surrounding these developments, see 'Why Buthelezi backed down', *Weekly Mail and Guardian* 22-28 April 1994.

be an election that he would lose, but lose in a quite remarkable manner.

As polling took place, allegations—some of them certainly justified—of widespread manipulation and fraud by Inkatha flew backwards and forwards. Monitors reported having been forced out of polling stations in kwaZulu; 'pirate' voting stations were set up by Inkatha; and ballot boxes were stuffed with Inkatha votes (at one counting station, 21 boxes were found neatly packed with ballots, impossible if they had been pushed through the narrow slots[28]). When the results of the election were reviewed by the Independent Electoral Commission, its head, Johan Kriegler, said that 'certain counting station data... could not be verified with the requisite degree of reliability.' However, as a result, after secret negotiations, it was decided that 'it would be a fair and reasonably reliable test of the votes of that province to adjust the verifiable information proportionately to the proven support of the respective parties'. After further negotiations it was decided to announce a technical victory for Inkatha, granting them a one seat majority in the kwaZulu/Natal legislature. Buthelezi was given a cabinet post, as Mandela had promised back in September 1993.[29]

Inkatha had won, but everyone knew, or thought they knew, that it had not really won. It therefore lacked the mandate to seek an independent Zulu State but could hardly disassociate itself from election results which left it controlling the kwaZulu/Natal region. This was breathtaking political daring on the part of the ANC leadership—daring that was repeated when it was declared that the ANC overall had fallen a fraction short of the necessary percentage to allow it to make the constitution without the support of other parties, while the NP had gained, by a tiny coincidental fraction, enough of the vote to entitle its leader to become one of the deputy presidents.

Probably never in the history of elections has blatant fiddling of the vote become a passport to peace and reconciliation.

Moreover, the result of the vote in the Western Cape, long predicted as it had been, produced another political irony. The extreme right had made all the running on the subject of Homelands for the whites,

---

28. For an account of this and other incidents, see 'Behind the great ballot box shuffle', *Weekly Mail and Guardian* 6-12 May 1994.
29. 'Violence and abuse dash peace hopes', *Guardian* 7 September 1993.

Conclusion

publicising its maps and arguing over ever more fantastic formulations of the all-white dream. In the end it was the NP which delivered, through the ballot box, the reality of a non-ANC 'homeland'. The Western Cape was won by the NP, largely with the votes of coloureds and with an NP stalwart of the old school, Hernus Kriel, installed as premier. Immediately this was seen as reassuring the irreconcilable whites—an area of South Africa would remain for the time being 'white'-controlled—and legitimately so.

So successful were these results in the short term in defusing political tension, that one cannot help wondering if similar 'solutions' might not help other of the world's troubled multi-ethnic states.

These events indicate the nature of the political dealing that underpinned the politics of change in South Africa after July 1993. Moreover, they were preceded and accompanied by vital declarations that white farmers would not lose their land and that the country's finances would continue to be controlled by the successful white minister Robert Keyes.[30] The rapid cessation of the worst township violence also left the academic fraternity suitably abashed. Violence turned out to have been political after all—not ethnic, or generational, or culturally rooted in African tradition.

2 WHAT IS ON OFFER FOR THE FUTURE?

This book was started before the Transitional Executive Council was established and continued through its deliberations and the run-up the elections in May. The world watched while the election was held.

The themes explored by Nico Steytler in his essay, written months before the election was held, have been shown by events to be relevant and well-judged. The deep political problems of determining the purpose of the election, who was to take part in it, and what its effect should or would be are well-anticipated.

It is significant that despite the overwhelming election success of the African National Congress, President Mandela took steps to ensure that

---

30. Mr Keys resigned unexpectedly during July 1994. His reasons were not made known to the public, but it rapidly became clear that they were personal, the event appeared to be without political significance, and the alarm reflected on the Johannesburg Stock Exchange was brief.

minority parties were brought into the new administration. There can be no doubt that the underlying philosophy was to draw the fires by co-opting those who were stoking them. Professor Steytler, writing in 1993, documented the steady retreat the National Government was forced to make from its initial position that the constitution should be settled first by a self-selected group of actors and thereafter tested by a referendum. What happened became history: in an election characterised by the drama of sheer joy in a genuine sense of freedom, with virtually no violence, and a degree of international attention and excitement which was certainly never parallelled in South African affairs even at their most violent, an election took place for an interim government and constitutional assembly. In the former role, an African National Congress-led government had the awesome task of laying the basis of a new social order and repairing and reconciling where apartheid had wrought havoc, destitution, and hatred. The foundations to be laid would be tested by the constitutional assembly: would the bi-cameral legislature sitting as one body be able to produce a constitution with which the people would be willing to enter the twenty-first century? The relationship between the two processes has been tense and dynamic; if President Mandela and his Government prove to be successful in the rebuilding of South Africa, then the first 'ordinary' election would be a confident step into the future. The importance of the election of 27-29 April 1994 and the installation of President Mandela on 10 May simply cannot be exaggerated, and South Africa and the world took note and took part with appropriate enthusiasm; but let it not be forgotten that these events had no greater purpose than to make hopes for the future possible—not certain. At his installation, President Mandela dedicated himself and his Government appropriately:

> Out of the experience of an extraordinary human disaster that lasted too long, must be born a society of which all humanity will be proud....
>
> Never, never and never again shall it be that this beautiful land will again experience the oppression of one by another and suffer the indignity of being the skunk of the world.

Conclusion

Any exegesis on these words would be superfluous or inappropriate. They can stand by themselves.

But comment is unavoidable. The audience—South Africans and the rest of the world alike—responded in various and contradictory ways. South Africa itself remained a divided nation still, and one would expect the President's words to have been greeted with varying levels of enthusiasm and scepticism. Certainly, the size of the vote at the election, the support for the African National Congress, and the jubilation of South Africans at the installation ceremony—attended as it was by the world's leaders—was on such a scale that one may feel secure in the conclusion that the majority of South Africans at the very least accepted the outcome on the basis that the past and present could only be improved on; and many looked forward to the future with confident certainty that it could only be better than the past. Certainly, the evidence was that those who would resist it ultimately with force were collapsing in disarray.

However, there was an industry of doubt already in production: its raw material an acknowledgement, implicit or explicit, of the dimensions of the task facing the new Government; and its products thereafter ranging from a sneer along the lines of 'Every black person will expect the Government to provide a house and a Mercedes', to the voicing of doubts whether anything will change at all, the apartheid regime having done no worse than could be expected and indeed making the best of the task.

The clearest mark of success will be when the *next* election takes place successfully. The Reconstruction and Development Programme (RDP) which the African National Congress-led Government adopted became central to creating the society in which this can happen. The RDP is described[31] as—

> an integrated, coherent socio-economic policy framework. It seeks to mobilise all our people and our country's resources toward the final eradication of apartheid and the building of a democratic, non-racial and non-sexist future.

It is a massive document, going far beyond the African National Congress's original election programme. Indeed, early in the text the point is stated bluntly: 'Making promises is easy—especially during

---

31. Reconstruction and Development Programme, Chapter 1, para. 1.1.1.

election campaigns—but carrying them out as a government is very much more difficult'.[32] It states that it was prepared in consultation with other mass organisations and research and non-governmental organisations, and calls for the involvement of key sectors such as the business community and their participation 'as fully as they may choose'. The Reconstruction and Development Programme is motivated by this spirit of inclusiveness:

> Those organisations within civil society that participated in the development of the Reconstruction and Development Programme will be encouraged by an African National Congress government to be active in and responsible for the effective implementation of the Reconstruction and Development Programme.[33]

It seems that, when one looks at the chapter headings of the Reconstruction and Development Programme, each of the themes in the preceding chapters of this book can be cross-referenced to it. Just a few instances will be noted here. Chapter 1 deals with the reasons for the need for a Reconstruction and Development Programme, and draws a succinct yet comprehensive picture of the principal features of South Africa: the contrast between poverty and degradation on the one hand, and wealth and advantage on the other. This is placed in the setting of a divided society, but not merely as a static consequence thereof. An effort is made to show that these problems, and the violence which emerged, are related dynamically to apartheid, and that addressing them requires as complex and inclusive a policy as apartheid itself once did when it was the motivation.

Chapter 1 sets out[34] six basic principles underlying the RDP, and explains their significance:

- ♦ An integrated and sustainable programme;
- ♦ A people-driven process;
- ♦ Peace and security for all;

---

32. N. 31, Chapter 1, para. 1.2.10.
33. N. 31, para. 1.1.5.
34. N. 31, para. 1.3.

Conclusion

♦ Nation-building;

♦ Link(ing) reconstruction and development;

♦ Democratisation of South Africa.

Chapter 2 is entitled 'Meeting Basic Needs', and starts with the question of poverty as the 'Problem Statement':

> Poverty is the single greatest burden of South Africa's people, and is the direct result of the apartheid system and the grossly skewed nature of business and industrial development which accompanied it....[35]

Ten basic priority areas are singled out in this chapter, and indeed the very first is land reform: the discussion of this topic by Andrew Caiger, and aspects of the tensions and pressures he explores, are picked up by the Reconstruction and Development Programme which describes land as the most basic need of rural dwellers.

A recurrent theme in all preceding chapters of this book is the development of a democratic tradition in South Africa. Chapter 5 of the Reconstruction and Development Programme concentrates on this. The chapter opens with a statement of the problems posed by the undemocratic past:

> The apartheid regime has been unrepresentative, undemocratic and highly oppressive. In past decades the state became increasingly secretive and militarised, and less and less answerable even to the constituency it claimed to represent.[36]

And almost immediately the RDP says bluntly, 'The People shall govern' and sets out a programme for the democratising of power: ensuring that the franchise is held and used by all, that elected structures function in an 'answerable and transparent' manner, and that civil society be developed to ensure that democracy '[does] not end with formal rights and periodic one-person, one-vote elections'.[37]

---

35. N. 31, para. 2.1.1.
36. N. 31, para. 5.1.1.
37. N. 31, paras. 5.2.1, 5.2.3, 5.2.6.

This chapter addresses the constituent assembly, national and provincial assemblies and governments, the security forces, the administration of justice, prisons, the public service, civil society, and other topics. In doing so, it reflects the observation it makes that 'Every aspect of South African life is deeply marked by minority domination and privilege'.[38]

Chapter 6 of the RDP examines its implementation. This calls for a 'thoroughgoing reform' of all parts of South Africa's 'excessively complex state system', and sets out in some detail what is envisaged. It is significant that it expresses anxiety to involve civil society—'parastatals, labour, civic and other organisations'.[39] The membership of COSATU, the 'civics', and religious, cultural, and even sports organisations amongst almost innumerable others in the now-defunct United Democratic Front foreshadowed the explicit inclusion of civil society in the RDP. This body, so central to the demise of the old order in its last years, has unquestionably cast its shadow across the RDP.

Chapter 7, the Conclusion, calls for contributions to the discussion and processes envisaged by the RDP in the spirit of its Introduction. It emphasises the need to encourage people 'to play an active role in implementing their own RDP with government assistance',[40] and its final words reflect what is clearly the motivating spirit:

> The future is in our hands and we must carry forward the work needed to finally liberate ourselves from the evils of apartheid.[41]

Only someone hankering after the past could fail to be moved by the Reconstruction and Development Programme. It is written in the same spirit as the Freedom Charter, which drove the struggle against apartheid from 26 June 1955. Cynics or sceptics may describe the RDP as naïve dreaming, but consider this in reply: South African political life has broken so many moulds; has been so daring, innovative, and indeed unpredictable; and shows such overwhelming needs and urgencies that can anyone wishing to retain credibility afford to be

---

38. N. 31, paras. 5.1.4.
39. N. 31, paras. 6.3.1.
40. N. 31, para. 7.5.
41. N. 31, para. 7.7.

Conclusion

cynical or sceptical?

The South African Government, led by President Mandela and the team he assembled about him, has strained every nerve to place the RDP in the hands of the people of South Africa. Should it once became their political property, it would seem that anything or anyone seeking to come between them and its realisation would be swept aside. The real test of the success of the RDP would be the *next* election; but it must be said that contemplating the consequences of failure makes the blood run cold. Let us put it more positively: the choices before South Africa have boiled down to a short list consisting of a single option, for the forces which brought the RDP into existence must and will bring it to success.

Index

Africanist 71, 142
African National Congress 5, 7, 8, 9, 15, 16, 20, 27, 28, 29, 31, 32, 33, 34, 36, 37, 40, 41, 42, 46, 47, 48, 49, 50, 51, 52, 53, 54, 55, 59, 60, 63, 64, 65, 66, 67, 68, 69, 70, 71, 72, 73, 74, 75, 77, 78, 79, 101, 102, 103, 105, 107, 108, 110, 111, 113, 114, 116, 124, 129, 130, 131, 132, 136, 137, 141, 147, 149, 177, 178, 179, 181, 182, 184, 185, 188, 189, 190, 191, 192
Afrikaans 57, 119
Afrikaner Resistance Movement 120, 183
Afrikaners 3, 4, 11, 12, 13, 14, 16, 20, 118, 178, 180, 182
agriculture 139
Angola 2, 8, 16, 186, 187
Angolan 17
apartheid 3, 4, 5, 6, 7, 9, 10, 16, 21, 22, 24, 25, 28, 29, 30, 31, 32, 37, 38, 39, 40, 43, 44, 45, 47, 50, 51, 55, 57, 58, 61, 69, 70, 71, 73, 75, 77, 78, 113, 119, 124, 180, 190, 191, 192, 193, 194
arbitration 145, 152, 168
arms 8, 17, 45, 54, 186
army 26, 35, 43, 45, 46, 48, 50, 54, 57, 179, 184
assassinations 31, 32, 45, 46, 49, 50, 51, 52, 55, 56, 58
attorneys 137, 147, 160, 161
AZAPO 141, 149
Azerbaijan 2

baaskap 4
ballot 17, 188, 189
Bangalore 87
bans 59
Bantu 5, 71
Bantustan 187 (*and see* Homelands)
Basutoland 10, 12
Beckett, Denis 36
Benoni 158
Bill of Rights 13, 14, 17, 18, 20, 21, 22, 81, 82, 100, 101, 102, 103, 104, 105, 106, 107, 108, 109, 110, 111, 112, 113, 114, 115, 116, 124, 126, 127, 130, 132, 133, 134, 136, 137, 138, 140, 182
Bisho 147, 158
Black Administration Act 116
'black on black' violence 3, 38, 39, 43, 44, 55
Bloemfontein 13, 56, 57
Boer War 178
Boipatong 34, 36, 37, 38, 46, 55, 59, 178
Boksburg 158
Bophutatswana 15, 65, 69, 70, 71, 120, 137, 150, 183, 185
Border-Ciskei 153, 157
Bosnia 16, 28
Botha, 'Pik' 29, 37, 43, 52, 177, 180
Botha, P.W. 7, 58, 183
bourgeoisie 180
boycott 141, 158, 187
Britain 1, 4, 5, 10, 11, 12, 13, 15, 16, 101, 186
bureaucracy 180, 184, 185

196

Index

burglary 60
business 56, 85, 87, 141, 151, 173, 174, 180, 192, 193
Buthelezi 6, 7, 13, 29, 32, 54, 180, 181, 182, 185, 187, 188

cabinet 4, 7, 59, 67, 72, 180, 181, 188
candidates 105, 169, 184
Cape 6, 10, 11, 12, 13, 14, 18, 20, 27, 41, 46, 118, 147, 153, 158, 159, 181, 182, 188, 189
Cape Town 27, 31, 41, 42
capital 127
capitalism 7
capitalist 4
capitals 13
chiefs 5, 15
child 34
children 12
church 3, 18, 24, 27, 44, 141, 149, 158
Ciskei 15, 65, 69, 70, 71, 150, 157, 158, 185
citizens 15, 69, 70, 82, 88, 109, 134, 148
citizenship 69, 70
civics 31, 158, 174, 194
Clocolan 58
CODESA 2, 14, 15, 63, 64, 65, 68, 70, 81, 124, 166, 181
Commonwealth 28, 77
Communism 1, 5, 8, 31, 47, 67, 177, 178
commuters 30
Comoros 8
confederalists 68
Confederation 10
Conservative Party 7, 65, 70, 180
consociationalism 65
constituency 12, 78, 149, 180
constituent assembly, *see* constitutional assembly
constitution 2, 4, 7, 10, 11, 12, 13, 14, 15, 16, 17, 18, 19, 20, 21, 23, 25, 61, 62, 63, 64, 65, 66, 67, 68, 69, 71, 75, 79, 81, 82, 83, 85, 86, 87, 88, 89, 90, 91, 92, 93, 94, 95, 96, 97, 98, 99, 100, 101, 102, 103, 104, 106, 107, 108, 109, 111, 125, 126, 127, 128, 129, 130, 132, 134, 135, 136, 138, 177, 178, 179, 180, 181, 182, 188, 190
constitutional assembly 15, 51, 62, 63, 64, 65, 66, 67, 68, 69, 70, 79, 81, 83, 100, 190, 194
convention 10, 13, 15, 63
COSAG 65, 70
COSATU 31, 170, 178, 194
courts 13, 14, 17, 18, 19, 20, 21, 22, 23, 62, 65, 71, 74, 75, 84, 85, 86, 87, 88, 89, 90, 91, 92, 93, 94, 95, 96, 97, 98, 99, 100, 101, 102, 103, 104, 105, 106, 107, 108, 109, 110, 111, 112, 119, 120, 121, 122, 123, 126, 127, 129, 130, 133, 134, 135, 136, 138, 143, 165, 166, 167, 182
crime 5, 23, 26, 28, 35, 39, 41, 42, 45, 47, 50, 51, 52, 54, 56, 57, 60, 77, 119, 120, 129, 143, 145, 160, 161, 162, 165, 184, 186
criminal gangs 56
Croat 28

Daveyton 34
Declaration of Human Rights 137
decolonisation 1, 2, 4, 126, 177
De Klerk 5, 6, 7, 10, 22, 24, 29, 43, 50, 51, 54, 58, 59, 64, 77, 81, 102, 115, 119, 141, 171, 177, 178, 179, 180, 181, 182, 183, 184, 185, 187
democracy 1, 17, 25, 30, 49, 55, 61, 62, 63, 64, 65, 66, 68, 69, 71, 72, 76, 77, 78, 79, 80, 81, 95, 109, 111, 114, 125, 135, 142, 173, 176, 177, 191, 193, 194
Diepsloot 119, 123
disenfranchised 69, 82, 133, 142
disguise 35, 52, 185, 187
Durban 27, 147
Dworkin 134

election 5, 6, 12, 13, 14, 15, 16, 17, 62, 65, 66, 67, 68, 69, 70, 71, 72, 73, 74,

75, 76, 77, 78, 80, 158, 160, 161, 177, 178, 181, 182, 183, 186, 187, 188, 189, 190, 191, 192, 193, 195
ethnic 2, 5, 6, 7, 11, 12, 13, 14, 16, 28, 29, 30, 37, 38, 39, 52, 66, 184, 186, 189
eviction 121, 122

facilitator 24, 148, 152, 157, 166
farm 21, 22, 57, 58, 114, 115, 117, 120, 121, 128, 139, 189
federalism 7, 13, 16, 65, 67, 68, 181, 182, 184, 185
firearms 35
freedom 18, 19, 31, 48, 65, 95, 109, 132, 135, 137, 182, 183, 184, 186, 190
Freedom Charter 114, 124, 194
freehold 21, 22, 117
Frelimo 9

Gandhi 91
gang 5, 7, 23, 41, 42, 53, 56, 187
Georgia 2
Germany 11, 79
Germiston 158, 159
Goldstone 24, 31, 35, 46, 48, 49, 50, 51, 54, 55, 56, 59, 61, 143, 146, 148, 149, 156, 179, 184, 186
Goniwe 47
Grahamstown 146, 158, 159
Griqualand 10
Group Areas Act 21, 125
grundnorm 62, 66

Hani 31
Hertzog 11
Hiemstra 137
Holomisa 71, 184
Homelands 4, 5, 6, 7, 11, 12, 13, 15, 16, 40, 64, 69, 70, 71, 78, 120, 123, 137, 180, 182, 183, 184, 185, 189
hostels 6, 23, 34, 36, 37, 54, 55, 61, 146, 147
Human Rights Commission 27, 32, 49, 51

IFP, *see* Inkatha Freedom Party
Independent Electoral Commission 188
Independent Forum for Electoral Education 72
India 4, 10, 18, 19, 21, 81, 82, 83, 84, 85, 87, 88, 89, 90, 91, 93, 94, 95, 96, 97, 98, 99, 100, 101, 102, 103, 104, 106, 107, 108, 109, 111, 112, 135, 179
Inkatha and Inkatha Freedom Party 6, 7, 15, 16, 23, 29, 32, 34, 35, 36, 37, 40, 41, 48, 49, 52, 53, 54, 56, 65, 66, 68, 78, 147, 170, 177, 179, 184, 185, 186, 187, 188
Internal Peace Institutions Act 23, 142, 147, 152, 159, 160, 161, 162, 170
Ireland 51
Israel 8

Johannesburg 27, 29, 30, 33, 35, 120, 147, 159
judges 75, 90, 91, 96, 101, 135
Justices of the Peace 154, 156, 160, 161, 162, 163, 164, 165, 166, 167, 168, 169, 171

Kaffraria 10
Keyes 189
Khayalitsha 42
Kriegler 188
Kriel 76, 189
Kroonstad 56
Krugersdorp 157
kwaMadala hostel 36, 37, 54
kwaZulu 6, 54, 65, 71, 147, 150, 185, 186, 187, 188

Land Acts 21, 114, 115, 117, 123
land reform 87, 114, 115, 124, 127, 139, 193
lawyers 19, 48, 89, 99, 145, 160, 169
Lebowa 185
legislature 11, 18, 83, 84, 86, 88, 89, 90, 97, 100, 120, 137, 188, 190
Local Peace Committees 24, 148, 152, 155, 162

Index

magistates 74, 156, 161, 164
majoritarianism 64, 78
Malan D.F. 14
Malan, Rian 36
Malawi 21, 127, 130, 136
Mandela 2, 5, 6, 47, 51, 59, 177, 178, 182, 188, 189, 190, 195
massacre 27, 32, 33, 34, 36, 37, 38, 44, 46, 52, 54, 55, 59, 147, 178
'medarb' 152, 167, 168
mediation 143, 146, 151, 152, 158, 159, 166, 167, 187
mercenary 8
Mozambique 2, 8, 9
multi-ethnic 2, 189
multi-nationalism 37

Namibia 8, 16, 35, 49, 53, 66, 121
Natal/kwaZulu 153, 156
nationalisation 91, 92
nationalism 4, 5, 8, 9, 12, 13, 14
National Party 4, 5, 6, 7, 11, 14, 15, 16, 25, 32, 38, 60, 65, 67, 76, 78, 105, 107, 147, 172, 178, 179, 180, 181, 185, 188, 189
National Peace Accord 2, 9, 23, 24, 25, 55, 61, 141, 142, 143, 144, 145, 146, 149, 151, 152, 156, 157, 159, 160, 166, 170, 171, 172, 174, 175, 176
National Peace Committee 24, 142, 143, 144, 146, 149, 158, 159, 171, 172; *and see* Peace Committees
National Peace Secretariat 24, 143, 145, 147, 148, 172
Nigeria 126
Nkomati 9

oaths 160, 161, 165
Orange Free State 10, 152

Pan-African Congress 5, 7, 15, 47, 58, 141, 149
Peace Accord, *see* National Peace Accord
Peace Committees (Local and Regional) 150, 152, 153, 154, 155, 156, 157, 158, 159, 169, 170, 171, 172, 173, 174

Peace Secretariat, *see* National Peace Secretariat
peacekeeping 143
Phalaborwa 150, 158
Phola Park 147
Pietermaritzburg 147
Pietersburg 158
police 6, 7, 23, 24, 26, 27, 28, 30, 31, 34, 35, 36, 40, 41, 42, 43, 45, 46, 47, 48, 51, 53, 54, 55, 56, 57, 59, 60, 61, 75, 76, 121, 122, 145, 146, 147, 156, 159, 161, 162, 164, 171, 175, 179, 183, 184, 185, 186
pollution 119
Port Elizabeth 27, 147
'Pretoria–Witwatersrand–Vereeniging Triangle' 33

quasi-federal 177
quitrent 117

railways 8, 35, 158
Ramaphosa 76
Ramushwana 184
Regional Peace Committees 145, 148, 152, 153
removal of population 21, 158
RENAMO 8, 9, 147, 187
Republic 10, 11, 12, 13, 49, 55, 183
Rhodesia 8, 11, 16

Saddam 56
Sarajevo 28
Serb 28
shebeen 5
Skweyiya 79
Slovo 67
Sotho 12
South African Broadcasting Corporation 77
South African Communist Party 5, 67, 177, 178
South African Defence Force 6, 9, 24, 35, 47, 49, 50, 76, 145, 179, 183, 184

199

South African Law Commission 101, 102, 105, 107, 108, 110, 111
Soweto 6, 34, 53, 142, 150
spoliation 121, 122, 123
squatting 21, 22, 33, 57, 109, 115, 117, 119, 121, 122, 123, 158

tribalism 3, 5, 12, 29, 38, 97

Uitenhage 162
United States of America 8

vigilantes 23, 32, 49
Volksfront 182
Volkstaat 182, 183

Zwelethini 187

www.ingramcontent.com/pod-product-compliance
Ingram Content Group UK Ltd.
Pitfield, Milton Keynes, MK11 3LW, UK
UKHW042121200326
4879IPUK00001B/1

9 780859 894593